# Dramas with a Message

## VOLUME THREE

Books by Doug Fagerstrom

*Baker Handbook of Single Adult Ministry* (gen. ed.)
*Counseling Single Adults* (gen. ed.)
*Dramas with a Message—Volume One*
*Dramas with a Message—Volume Two*
*Dramas with a Message—Volume Three*
*The Lonely Pew* (with Jim Carlson)
*Single Adult Ministry, the Second Step* (gen. ed.)
*Single to God* (gen. ed.)
*Single to Single* (gen. ed.)
*Singles Ministries Handbook* (gen. ed.)
*Worship and Drama Library, volume 15*

# Dramas with a Message

21 Reproducible Dramatic
Sketches for the Local Church

## VOLUME THREE

# DOUG FAGERSTROM

kregel
PUBLICATIONS

Grand Rapids, MI 49501

*Dramas with a Message: 21 Reproducible Dramatic Sketches for the Local Church—Volume Three*

© 1999 by Doug Fagerstrom

Published by Kregel Publications, a division of Kregel, Inc., P.O. Box 2607, Grand Rapids, MI 49501. Kregel Publications provides trusted, biblical publications for Christian growth and service. Your comments and suggestions are valued.

For more information about Kregel Publications, visit our web site: www.kregel.com

Cover photo: © PhotoDisc
Cover design: Nicholas G. Richardson
Book design: Kevin Ingram

**Library of Congress Cataloging-in-Publication Data**
Fagerstrom, Douglas L.
Dramas with a message: 21 reproducible dramatic sketches for the local church—volume one / Doug Fagerstrom.
        p.    cm.
   1. Drama in public worship. 2. Drama in Christian education. 3. Christian drama, American. I. Title.
BV289F34         1999         246'.72—dc21         99-43099
                                                                         CIP

ISBN 0-8254-2581-6 (v. 1)
ISBN 0-8254-2582-4 (v. 2)
ISBN 0-8254-2583-2 (v. 3)

*Printed in the United States of America*
1 2 3 4 5 / 03 02 01 00 99

# A Note to the Drama Director

*Dramas with a Message* is designed for the worship service or special program in local churches or ministries. Sketches are short—about five to seven minutes in length. Stage set-up is simple, often needing only a chair, table, or hand props, and you are permitted to photocopy as many scripts as you need. Actors can be inexperienced, since the characters and lines come out of everyday events.

Some sketches are comical (although that is not their primary purpose), some are serious, and some have an ending that will surprise the audience. All of them carry simple themes. They are not complicated with hidden messages or deep theological truths. While the dramas can stand alone, they often work better as illustrations in a service or program. Not every sketch attempts to deliver an entire message. Some leave the audience "hanging" and in need of a speaker to complete the point. You, the director, will determine how best to fit a sketch into its context.

Know your audience. Know the message for the program. Know your actors. Select the right sketch—and then, have fun! Enjoy the sketches. Build a team of actors and support staff who will value being part of a ministry that delivers biblical principles and truths in an entertaining way.

Blessings as you share the message of Good News through these dramas.

DOUG FAGERSTROM

# Acknowledgments

These sketch volumes are dedicated to the faithful actors and actresses at Calvary Church who volunteer their time and talent and have graciously performed these sketches at the "Saturday Night" ministry, each and every week.

# Contents

Forgive You? Never!

## THEME

Forgiveness is difficult for everyone, especially those who have not experienced the forgiveness of Jesus Christ. This sketch shares the struggle and the difficulty in being able to forgive others.

## CHARACTERS

HARVEY: Self-righteously thinks he has put the past behind him, not facing up to the hurt he caused Wynan thirty-seven years ago when he "stole" Wynan's true love. Dress is casual attire.

WYNAN: He has bitterly refused to forgive Harvey for thirty-seven years. Their encounter in the grocery store is not a welcome sight. He is dressed in very sloppy attire.

## SETTING

Ideally, each one is pushing a shopping cart (borrowed, with permission, from a local supermarket) containing a few grocery items.

*Both men are moving from stage back to stage front, pushing their carts.
Wynan is miserably grumbling, and Harvey is trying to sing or whistle
a cheerful tune. As they move stage front, without ever seeing each other,
they turn into each other, and the dialogue begins.*

HARVEY:     *[trying to be chipper, with a touch of cynicism]* Well, good morning, Wynan! Fancy meeting you.

WYNAN:      I thought you were dead! *[quickly turns and mumbles under breath]* At least I wish you were.

HARVEY:     Ah, I didn't quite hear what you just said.

WYNAN:      Harvey . . . I said, I wish you were dead! There, I said it, you heard it, and I have groceries to buy.

HARVEY:     You just can't let go of it, can you, Wynan? How long has it been? . . . thirty . . . thirty-five years?

WYNAN:      *[looks directly at Harvey for the first time]* It has been thirty-seven years, Harvey Johnson . . . and . . . and you know it.

9

HARVEY:    Wynan, I put that behind me years ago. I'm sorry you couldn't.

WYNAN:    Oh, Mr. "Righteous" . . . Mr. "Put-It-Behind-You." Well, easy for you to say. You got Martha, and I got nothing but grocery shopping for thirty-seven years by myself. That means [yells] alone, Harvey!

HARVEY:    [conciliatory] Look, Wynan, what happened, happened.

WYNAN:    [mocks] What happened, happened. [angry] Because you made it happen . . . you . . . you thief.

HARVEY:    Thief? I told you then, Wynan, and I am going to tell you again. I did not steal Martha away from you. She . . . [a bit arrogant] she just saw a better thing and . . . went for it. And that is history, and you can't rewrite history.

WYNAN:    Harvey, Martha was my life, and I loved her more than anything. And when she left to go with you . . . well, you might as well have put a bullet right here. [points to forehead] I will never be able to forgive you, Harvey Johnson. You hurt me bad. Real bad. But what do you care?

HARVEY:    Wynan, what can I say to you? Martha is gone now, and it is just you and me in this little town. I see you, and you see me, and we keep avoiding each other. . . . Just tell me, what can I say to make this go away?

WYNAN:    Harvey, there is nothing you can say to make this go away. There is nothing anyone can say to make me feel better. And if there is a God, there is nothing He could say to make me feel better. But, it wouldn't hurt for you to say you are sorry. [dead silence between them as they uncomfortably look at each other] Well, I'm listening.

HARVEY:    [upset] Look, I told you, this was not my . . . [catches himself, pauses, says sincerely] All right . . . all right . . . I'm sorry. There, I said it.

WYNAN:    [skeptically] I wish I could believe you.

HARVEY:    [angry] You just told me to tell you—

WYNAN:    Trust, Harvey. The issue is trust. I guess I just don't know if I could ever trust you again. Heh, to think you were my best friend.

HARVEY:    [a bit lighter] We had some good laughs, didn't we?

WYNAN:    Remember Old Man MacIntyre and the eggs we threw at his front door? [both start to chuckle] Got him right in the old bread basket when he opened it . . . didn't know he was home.

HARVEY:    [laughing] No, we didn't. [laughter dies]

WYNAN:      Wait a minute, what are we doing laughing? I am supposed to be mad at you.

HARVEY:     Each to their own, Wynan, each to their own.

WYNAN:      *[reflective]* I guess I can't ever get that day out of my mind when Martha told me she loved you more than me.

HARVEY:     *[sincere]* What can I do for you, Wynan?

WYNAN:      *[matter-of-factly]* You know, you could pick up the phone and call me sometime.

HARVEY:     You . . . would like me to call you?

WYNAN:      *[tender]* Sure, why not? If anything, I would love to hear some Martha stories.

HARVEY:     I'll call you, Wynan. I'll call you.

WYNAN:      *[looks into Harvey's cart]* You know, Harvey, you got enough cholesterol in that cart to kill a mule.

HARVEY:     Yeah? Well, I'm surprised you can even push your cart with all of that junk food in there.

*[They begin to push their carts away from each other.]*

WYNAN:      *[lighthearted]* You're hopeless, Harvey . . . hopeless.

HARVEY:     *[spirited]* I'll call you, Wynan. I'll call you.

2

Forgive...
Me

## THEME

Forgiveness is difficult when another hurts us. Forgiveness is just as difficult when we make choices that inflict pain on ourselves. In other words, it is not any easier to forgive ourselves than to forgive others, as we will see in this sketch.

## CHARACTERS

LINDA: Represents anyone who has made tragic mistakes in life. She is dressed semi-casually.

BARBARA: The local manicurist. She is dressed casually with a smock over her clothes.

## SETTING

A small table for manicures and two chairs facing each other at stage center.

*Barbara and Linda are seated as dialogue begins.*

BARBARA: *[friendly, trying to get a conversation going]* So, how was your _____? *[name a holiday or special event]*

LINDA: *[preoccupied]* Fine . . . hassle free. Now be sure these nails are perfect. *[nervous]* I can't have anything go wrong.

BARBARA: *[trying to be lighthearted]* Oh, I sense a special date coming up.

LINDA: No, Barbara, it's not what you think.

BARBARA: *[still trying]* No special date? Let me see, you are going to have your hair done next. I sense a new dress in your future, and you are telling me "no special date."

LINDA: No date, Barbara.

BARBARA: *[excited]* You are getting Nurse of the Year! Congratulations!

LINDA: *[laughs]* Ha! I will be lucky if I still have a job, with last month's review and a string of absentee days.

BARBARA: *[realizes she hit a nerve]* Whoa, sorry. I didn't know things were tough at work. So, what is the special occasion?

LINDA: You really need to know, don't you?

BARBARA: Look, you are talking to the original subscriber to the *National Inquirer*. *[direct]* Tell me what is going on.

LINDA: Can I trust you to not broadcast this all over town?

BARBARA: Girl Scouts honor.

LINDA: I am going to meet my daughter for the first time.

BARBARA: *[yells]* Your daughter?!

LINDA: Shhh! You promised not to broadcast this all over.

BARBARA: Yeah, but, you never told me you had a daughter.

LINDA: There is a lot you don't know about me.

BARBARA: Linda, how long have we known each other?

LINDA: Since I moved to town. About fifteen years.

BARBARA: How come you never told me you had a daughter?

LINDA: Well, like I said, there are a lot of things you don't know about me, and that is one that I am . . . not very proud of.

BARBARA: *[awkward]* And, your daughter's father . . .

LINDA: I don't even know his name.

BARBARA: I'm sorry, Linda. I never had a clue.

LINDA: *[a bit reminiscent]* My mother said I was young and foolish, and my dad's response was to throw me out of the house.

BARBARA: So, you have had it rough. Have you seen your parents since?

LINDA: Never saw them again, and I never saw my baby. Just heard a faint cry in the emergency room where I delivered after I ran my car off the road.

BARBARA: How come you have never shared your story?

LINDA: How can I? The guilt and the pain are what I live with every day. It is not a pretty picture and, besides, people would only think the worst of me.

BARBARA: But, Linda, you need to forgive yourself. You can't keep on with all that hurt.

LINDA: Barbara, I can't forgive my parents, or my child's father. And I can't forgive my own sister . . . who gave up on me. How am I ever going to forgive me?

BARBARA: I know I don't have all the answers, but you are going to have to let go of all that happened in the past and move on. *[a bit more intense]* You have got to let go, girl, and leave the past behind you.

LINDA: *[wanting to agree]* You have been a good friend, Barbara, but I just don't think I know how to forgive. *[Barbara inflicts a little pain while manicuring.]* Ouch! Take it easy, I only have ten of those.

BARBARA: *[compassionate]* Oooo, I am so sorry.

LINDA: That's okay . . . don't worry about it. You usually wound me once a month.

BARBARA: Hey, you just did it.

LINDA: Did what?

BARBARA: You forgave me. You let go of something that I did to you that really hurt.

LINDA: But this is a finger.

BARBARA: And she is your daughter. Now, you need to let go of whatever you did to yourself, and the choices you made to cause all of this pain, and make your first visit with your daughter the best it can be.

LINDA: Do you really think I can?

BARBARA: With God's help, I know you can!

**3**

*Hush, Little Baby*

## THEME

Most everyone wants to believe that the story of Cinderella will be theirs. Of course, that was a fairy tale, and so is the dream of modern day Cinderellas. The all-American dream is a myth, as we see in this sketch.

## CHARACTERS

MOTHER: Tries to make life perfect for her daughter, as she tries to make sure that the best will happen. Scene 1, Mother is a new mom with a tiny baby. Scene 2, she is a bit older and wiser. Her dress is casual in both scenes, showing a change of clothes between scenes.

JILL: (daughter in scene 2) A young adult woman who is trying to find answers to an already difficult life. Her losses are many. Her pain has been too much for her age. She seeks the counsel of her mother.

## SETTING

Scene 1: Mother stands or sits in a rocker stage center with her new-born baby (a doll wrapped in a pink blanket).

Scene 2: Mother and daughter have coffee at a small café table.

## SCENE 1

*Music is playing the tune "Hush, Little Baby, Don't You Cry" as mother walks out stage center with a baby wrapped in a blanket. A crying baby background tape would be an excellent sound effect.*

MOTHER: *[singing to her baby]* Hush, little baby, don't say a word, Mama's going to buy you a mocking bird. And if that mocking bird don't sing, Mama's gonna buy you a diamond ring. And if that diamond ring don't shine, Mama's gonna buy you a . . .

*[speaks with great hope and joy]* Oh, little Jill, you are the most wonderful gift that God could have ever given me. And you are going to have a perfect life. Yes, Mama's going to see to it that you get the finest education, you will have the best piano teacher in the county, and tap dance lessons will begin at age three. Yes, you will have the best of everything . . . anything your heart desires. And if you want to be a cheerleader, or date the captain of the football team, you just let your mama know, and you will have what you want. You, your daddy, and I will travel to the most exciting places in the world, and we will be the family that lives happily ever after.

[with tender optimism] I can see it in your eyes, Jill, a whole world of opportunity awaits you, and you are going to have it all. You are a lucky little girl, Jill, a lucky little girl. [sings] "Now little baby close your eyes, Mama's going to give you a paradise."

[Mother and baby exit.]

## SCENE 2

*Mother and Jill are seated at a café table drinking coffee.*

JILL: [reflecting] Mom, I remember when we used to come here as a family. I thought you and Dad were really cool because anybody who was anybody would come here for lunch or dinner.

MOTHER: Those were fun days, weren't they, Jill?

JILL: [serious tone] Mom, what really happened with you and Dad?

MOTHER: [saddened] I guess you would say we just lost what we once had.

JILL: But you seemed so happy, and we had such great times as a family.

MOTHER: I know, honey, but you need to know that a lot of what you saw was just for you and your brother. Your dad and I just got further apart, and we couldn't put it back together.

JILL: [straightforward] You know, I was really mad at you for leaving Daddy when I was just starting high school.

MOTHER: I know, Jill, I know. [awkward pause] Could we talk about . . . about something else? It is a nice day, and this is your birthday.

JILL: [trying to be positive] You're right, Mom. How is your new job going?

MOTHER: Let's try another category.

JILL: [amusing] Okay, Mom, for $50 let's try . . . current events. Any new boyfriends?

MOTHER: Wait a minute, that is supposed to be my question to you.

JILL: I asked you first.

MOTHER: I'm older.

JILL: It's my birthday.

MOTHER: And you want it to be a good one.

JILL: Okay, Mom, how's my kid brother doing?

MOTHER: I wish I could tell you. I got a card from him about two months ago, and it was postmarked somewhere in Montana. All he said was, "Almost out of money, Mom." And to think I was going to write him the same card. *[light laugh, trying to brighten the mood]* Well, tell me about my granddaughter. Is she still playing the piano?

JILL: She still plays, Mom. *[a bit upset]* But if Terry doesn't come up with some more child support, the lessons will have to go. He has been such a jerk.

MOTHER: Oh, I wish you could just move back here and stay with me for a while, until you got back on your feet.

JILL: I can't, Mom, you know that. Terry has me stuck in North Dakota, and if I try to leave with Tessa, he will get custody of her, and I am not going to lose my daughter to that two-timing, no-good . . .

MOTHER: Listen, I have a few dollars I can start sending you. When your grandma died in June, I received a little money, and I can—

JILL: Mom, no, you have done enough. . . . *[pause, drinks coffee, very serious]* Mom?

MOTHER: Yes, Jill?

JILL: Remember that song you used to sing to me all the time about the mocking bird and diamond ring and how life was going to be wonderful?

MOTHER: I'm afraid I do, Jill. I'm afraid I do.

JILL: How come none of that ever came true? Is life really that unfair?

MOTHER: I think it is, Jill . . . I just didn't know any better then. And no one seemed to have any answers for me.

JILL: Mom, where was God in all of this?

MOTHER: I don't know, Jill. I don't know.

JILL: Do you think that if we did know, life would have been any different?

*[Music plays as they hold hands and lights go out.]*

Graduation Grief

4

## THEME

Forgiveness and grief battle one another after we experience rejection and hurt in our lives from others. It seems that the ones closest to us hurt us the most. That is when forgiveness is most needed.

## CHARACTERS

TOM: In scene 1, he is a young man graduating from college. He wears a graduation gown. Scene 2 takes place thirteen years later. As a married man, Tom is still bitter that his father did not come to his graduation. He is dressed casually.

SUSAN: Tom's girlfriend in scene 1, is all dressed up for Tom's graduation party. In scene 2, she is dressed casually as Tom's wife.

## SETTING

Scene 1: Outdoors after the graduation ceremony. An open stage.
Scene 2: Tom and Susan's living room, with a couch, end table, and phone.

## SCENE 1

*Tom and Susan are standing center stage. Tom is gripping his diploma with a smile on his face.*

TOM: *[excited]* Well, I got it!

SUSAN: Congratulations, Tom! I am so proud of you.

TOM: *[looking around]* Ah, Susan, have you seen him yet?

SUSAN: *[conciliatory]* Tom, that is the fifth time you have asked me in the last ten minutes. And no, I haven't seen him. But, don't worry. Maybe he ran into some problems and, well—

TOM: *[trying hard to believe Susan]* Yeah, busy . . . he is real busy.

SUSAN: *[trying to change the atmosphere]* Let's go to your apartment. Maybe he went straight to your graduation party.

TOM: *[happy]* Right, you are right. I'll bet he is already there. *[lighthearted]* A real party animal . . . that guy. *[convincing himself]* Yeah, come on, let's go.

*[Tom starts to exit, but Susan pulls him back.]*

SUSAN:     Tom?

TOM:        What Susan?

SUSAN:     What about them? *[She points to the audience.]*

TOM:        What about them?

SUSAN:     It would be rude not to invite them, wouldn't it?

TOM:        To the party? My graduation party? They don't even know me!

SUSAN:     I know, but they look kind of hungry, and I am sure that some of them would love a free meal . . .

TOM:        And did you order enough food for _____ *[number of people in audience]* people?

SUSAN:     No . . . I just thought—

TOM:        Susan! *[turns to audience, rather embarrassed and apologetic]* Sorry, folks, it's not going to work out this time—

*[Susan whispers something to Tom.]*

TOM:        *[to Susan]* Okay. *[to audience]* Okay, welcome to _____ *[name of program]*.


# SCENE 2

*Tom is sitting in a chair by a phone looking rather miserable as he stares at the floor. Susan comes walking in, looks at Tom, folds arms, pauses, and speaks.*

SUSAN:     Tom, just pick up the phone and call him.

TOM:        No way! I am not making the first move.

SUSAN:     *[trying to encourage]* But you know you want to.

TOM:        No, I don't, and no I won't. It's not going to happen, Susan.

SUSAN:     *[upset with Tom]* All right, all right, just sit there. . . . You know you are just as stubborn as he is.

*[Susan exits.]*

TOM: *[mocks]* Stubborn as he is. I'll show you stubborn. *[looks up, as if talking to God]* Look, this is not fair. *[pause]* He started this whole mess. *[pause]* And You know it! . . . At least You should. *[wondering]* I think You should . . . ah, do You even know what I'm talking about? *[a bit intimidated]* All right, no offense, I was just checking. *[pause, as if listening]* You want me to what? You know, You sound just like my wife.

SUSAN: *[comes back into room, looking very pleased with Tom]* Tom, I am so proud of you!

TOM: *[puzzled]* What do you mean?

SUSAN: Well, I heard you talking in here. You did call, didn't you?

TOM: *[silent]*

SUSAN: Tom?

TOM: *[almost defiant]* No, I didn't call.

SUSAN: Then who were you talking to?

TOM: Ah, . . . my Fa . . . ther.

SUSAN: Then you did call!

TOM: No. I didn't call. God. My Father God. I was talking to Him!

SUSAN: *[somewhat pleased]* Well, what did He have to say?

TOM: You guys are in this together, aren't you? *[Susan smiles.]* Okay, He said the same thing you have been saying. *[irritated]* But, Susan, he didn't come to my graduation. And now getting sick is his own fault, not mine!

SUSAN: Tom, it has been thirteen years . . . and he could die. Please pick up the phone and call him.

*[Susan exits offstage.]*

TOM: *[slowly picks up the phone and dials from a small piece of paper in his pocket]* Hi, . . . Mom? Oh, I'm sorry, nurse, ah, this is Tom Johnson, could I speak to my dad? *[anxious pause]* Hello, Dad? T . . . Tom, your son, Dad. *[big breath]* Dad, I want to say that I—what? Oh, Dad, I didn't think you remembered. I've forgotten all about that. *[looks up with a guilty response]* Hey, it was a lousy graduation party anyway. Yeah, all these people from church showed up, trashed the place, and we ran out of food. *[pause]* Dad, you're kidding? Look, you don't need to apologize. *[bewildered]* I had no idea! Listen, would it be okay with you if I flew out to see you this weekend? Great! *[pause]* Me too, Dad . . . love ya. Bye. *[hangs up phone then looks up]* Hey, thanks!

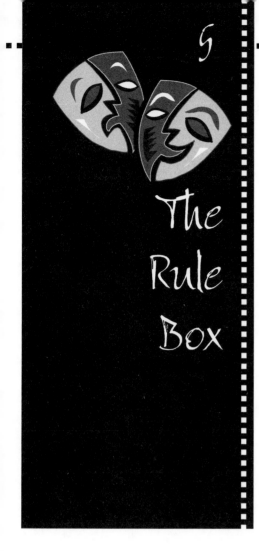

## The Rule Box

## THEME

God gave us spiritual rules for living in His Word, the Bible. Rules that, with His help, set us free. However, religious leaders often add their own rules and requirements to help people be "right" with God, weighing them down with unnecessary burdens.

## CHARACTERS

BENNY GOODMAN: An aggressive salesman who sells Holy Boxes with everything needed for a good spiritual life. He is dressed in a brightly colored suit, tie, and shirt.

BOB: Trying to get his spiritual life together but struggling. He is dressed rather casually.

LOVELY LADY: Represents a fundamental temptation. She is an attractive woman, well dressed, sitting on a park bench reading a small paperback. She responds with a subtle annoyance over Benny's and Bob's actions.

## SETTING

A small stand for a street vendor at stage right. The stand is set up with a sign that says "Righteousness for Sale." The stand should be very simple with a couple of small, plain, white boxes available and a long belt. One is lettered "Holy Box." Inside this box are the following props: sunglasses, roll of masking tape, gloves, earphones, length of rope. There is also a park bench at stage left.

*Benny comes out to his stand, and Lovely Lady walks out to sit on park bench. She begins to read her book or magazine. Bob comes walking up to Benny's stand.*

BENNY: *[flamboyant]* Hello, hello, hello! What a bea-u-ti-ful day. *[coyly]* And how can I help you with your . . . spiritual life?

BOB: *[naive]* Well, I saw your sign and figured that maybe I could use some help in that area. You know, the God-stuff, religion, do good, eternal life . . . you know, all that holy stuff.

BENNY: *[puts his arm around Bob]* My boy, you have come to the right place! *[hyped]* Why for only $99.99 I can fix you up with everything that will make your life holy, religious, and everything that you have always wanted.

BOB: *[excited]* Wow, only $99.99?

BENNY: You will be the envy of everyone in your office and neighborhood.

BOB: *[reaches for money]* Here, keep the change.

BENNY:    [sarcastically] A penny. Oh, thank you, thank you so much.

BOB:    [naive] Don't mention it.

BENNY:    Don't worry, I won't.

BOB:    [curious] Now what do I do?

BENNY:    Just wear this box for the rest of your life and use the contents every day. [straps on Holy Box with a belt around Bob's chest, so that the box is now on his back]

BOB:    [a bit disappointed] Everywhere? Every day?

BENNY:    You want to be religious and holy, don't you?

BOB:    Well . . . yeah, I do. I think. . . .

BENNY:    Then what a small price to pay!

BOB:    But, how does it work?

BENNY:    Simple, boy, simple! See that over there? [points to Lovely Lady on bench]

BOB:    Boy, do I! Wow!

BENNY:    [reaches in box and pulls out a pair of dark glasses] You can't look, boy, you just can't look and be a righteous man.

BOB:    [groping in blindness] Hey, I can't see anything!

BENNY:    The box works, doesn't it? Now you are just a little more righteous.

BOB:    Can't I just go over there and . . . and . . . shake her hand?

BENNY:    [reaches in box for a pair of gloves and puts them on Bob] You can't touch either, boy. Now you are on your way to being holy.

BOB:    [discouraged] Thanks a lot. Well, just direct me over to the bench, so I can at least sit next to her. You never know, we might have a lot in common.

BENNY:    [reaches in box for a rope and ties Bob's legs together] I am sure glad you bought the deluxe Holy Box. You can't move, boy, you just have to stay put to be a holy man.

BOB:    [innocent] I just wanted to talk—

BENNY:    Talk?! [reaches in box for tape] Just wanted to talk. You just don't get it, do you, Bob? [tapes Bob's mouth shut] You can't talk either, boy, if you are going to be the saint of saints.

BOB: *[mumbles through tape]*

BENNY: *[looks at Bob]* I sense some angry thoughts, son. *[reaches in box for earphones to put on Bob]* You can't think that way, boy. A saint just can't think! *[Benny looks over Bob, up and down.]* Well, you should make it now. You are a righteous, holy saint!

*[Benny exits.]*

LOVELY LADY: *[annoyed by the commotion, gets up, and walks past Bob and looks at him with disgust]* What a sick-o! *[to audience]* You know, some people will do just about anything.

*[Lovely Lady exits. Music comes up and Bob hops offstage.]*

# Row, Row, Row your Own Boat

## THEME

The nuclear family is disappearing from our culture, at least in function. The younger generation is picking up bad habits as it must deal with the shortcomings of the non-nuclear family. This sketch shows a father and son who neglect their relationship through the years, and how it affects the next generation.

## CHARACTERS

DAD: A typical all-American dad, which makes him too busy, tense, and preoccupied. He is wearing fishing clothes/gear.

SON [BILLY]: A typical son with dreams, hopes, and high expectations. He is wearing summer play clothes and is eight years old in scene 1. He is eighteen years old in scene 2. In scene 3, Bill is twenty-eight years old and thirty-eight years old in scene 4. An adult should play the role in all four scenes.

GRANDSON [BOBBY]: A pre- or early adolescent. He should not be an adult playing the role of a child. He is wearing shorts, T-shirt, and a baseball cap.

## SETTING

A row boat is on the platform as if it were in the water, with fishing poles and some tackle.

*Director's Note: Some time should elpase between the four scenes. Do not attempt to run them one immediately after another. In fact, it may be wise to show the audience a placard indicating the number of years that have elapsed between scenes.*

## SCENE 1

*Billy and Dad are in the boat. Dad looks like he has lost his last friend. He is rather short-tempered and obviously preoccupied.*

BILLY: Hey, Daddy, I just put the worm on the hook by myself, see? What now, Daddy?

DAD: *[not even looking]* Throw it in the water.

BILLY: *[still excited]* Okay, Daddy. It's in the water. Now what do I do?

DAD: *[preoccupied]* Wait, boy . . . wait.

BILLY: *[long pause, funny antics, then sings]* Row, row, row your boat, gently down the street. . . . *[laughing]* Hey, Daddy, did you hear me? I said street instead of stream—

DAD: *[short and abrupt]* I heard you and so did all of the fish. I think it is getting late, Son, and . . . I have a lot to do at the house. Let's go.

BILLY: But Daddy, you promised we would go fishing all day today, and I really want to stay and catch—

DAD: Pull in your line, boy. We're going home.

*[freeze; blackout]*

## SCENE 2

*Ten years later. Dad and Billy are in the fishing boat. Billy is not real interested in fishing. Dad is trying hard to communicate.*

DAD: *[optimistically]* Hey, Billy, catch any fish yet?

BILLY: *[bored silly]* Do you see or smell any fish?

DAD: Sorry, Billy, I just thought that maybe . . .

BILLY: Dad, if I catch any fish, you will be the first to know, and it's "Bill," Dad, not "Billy."

DAD: Right, Son . . . ah, Bill. *[uncomfortable pause]* How was your last semester at the university?

BILLY: You know, I have to be back home in about an hour. Sandra is picking me up.

DAD: Sure, Son, we don't want to disappoint Sandra. Maybe we can do this . . . again some time.

BILLY: *[reeling in line]* Dad, I'm ready to go.

DAD: Yeah . . . me too.

*[freeze; blackout]*

## SCENE 3

*Ten years later. Dad and Bill are in the fishing boat. Bill is approaching middle age, and Dad is getting on in years.*

DAD: *[irritated]* I don't know why you dragged me out here in this damp cold.

BILL: *[equally upset]* Me? This was your harebrained idea. I told you to give it a rest. You know I hate fishing.

DAD: Hate fishing? Since when? You would go fishing twenty-four hours a day, seven days a week when you were a kid. I had to drag you out of the boat to go home.

BILL: And, Dad, you did a fine job dragging me around. Let's just give it up and go home. You have your life, and I have mine. We are not kidding anyone out here in this leaking tub of a boat.

DAD: Throwing in the towel already, huh?

BILL: *[bitter]* You taught me well.

DAD: *[defensive]* I see, now this is all my fault.

BILL: See, that is what you always do. Either the martyr or the executioner.

DAD: Thank you, Son, for that fine evaluation. I will be sure to put you on my résumé as a reference.

BILL: *[pause]* What do you want from me?

DAD: *[humbled]* Just a son . . . just a . . . son.

BILL: Maybe you should have thought about that a long time ago.

*[freeze; blackout]*

## SCENE 4

*Bill and Bobby are now in the boat. Bill is sitting where his dad used to sit, and Bobby is sitting where Bill used to sit.*

BOBBY: *[with great curiosity]* Hey, Daddy?

BILL: *[preoccupied]* Yes, Son?

BOBBY: Do fish really like to eat worms?

BILL: I don't know, Son. I guess so.

BOBBY: *[pause, starts singing]* Row, row, row your boat gently down the . . . street. *[starts laughing]* Ha, ha . . . hey, Daddy—

BILL: Yes, Bobby, you sang street instead of stream. Are you about done?

BOBBY:   But Daddy, we just got here, and this is our every other Saturday. Besides, I don't want to go back to Mom's yet.

BILL:   Why not? I thought you liked it better at Mom's.

BOBBY:   *[saddened]* Not really. I don't like her new boyfriend, and he is always pushing me away. *[Bill uncomfortably looks away.]* Daddy?

BILL:   *[frustrated]* What now, Bobby?

BOBBY:   Are you and Mom ever going to get back together?

BILL:   Only God knows that, Son.

BOBBY:   Daddy?

BILL:   What is it with all the questions? Look, one more question, then we're going.

BOBBY:   Okay, Daddy, but if only God knows, then why doesn't He tell us? I think He wants us to be a family again because that is what I really want. . . . So, Daddy, *[pause, no response]* would you ask God to tell us when we can be a family again . . . please?

*[freeze; blackout]*

## THEME

"Everyone lies" is the excuse we hear and use. Lies have taken on a proportional standard, so a small lie is okay but a big lie isn't. But lies can be subtle, as in half-true statements or half-hearted promises. Any lie causes pain and certain damaging consequences, as this sketch reveals.

## CHARACTERS

TIM: A self-proclaimed ladies' man. He finds himself in big trouble through his lies, but he never learns his lesson. He is dressed in the latest casual style.

JODY: The innocent, naive young woman who buys into all of Tim's lies. She soon discovers the truth and erupts. She is dressed casually.

DAVE: Tim's roommate who unknowingly blows Tim's cover. He is dressed in contemporary/casual attire.

ANGIE: Jody's friend who loves a good round of gossip. She is also dressed casually.

VOICE-OVER #1: Movie announcer

VOICE-OVER #2: TV announcer

## SETTING

Stage Right: Tim and Dave's apartment, a real bachelor's pad with a couch.
Stage Left: A row of chairs representing a movie theater.

## SCENE 1

*Tim is sitting on the couch trying hard to impress Jody, who is seated next to him.*

TIM: *[gushy, melodramatic]* Jody, I just want you to know that no one has made me feel the way that you do.

JODY: *[embarrassed, but impressed]* Oh, Tim, you are so sweet.

TIM: Really, Jody, I can't remember when I have dated someone as wonderful as you. You are kind, sweet, and . . . gorgeous. Why, life would come to a screeching halt if you were not a part of my life.

JODY: Well, Tim, you know that I feel the same way about you. In fact, I was wondering—

TIM:    Wonder no more—you are the only one, Jody. I have not looked at another woman in . . . at least three months since we have been seeing each other.

JODY:   It has been six months, Tim.

TIM:    See what I mean . . . ah, you have been so wonderful that six months seems like only three months. The time, yes, the time has gone by far too quickly. You have just caused me to forget that there are any other women on planet earth.

[Dave enters stage right and comes into the apartment on Tim's last line.]

DAVE:   Hey, I heard that!

[startles/embarrasses Tim and Jody]

TIM:    [jumps to his feet] Ah, Dave, thanks for knocking.

DAVE:   I do live here, you know.

TIM:    [back to impressing Jody] Well, Dave, let me introduce you to—

DAVE:   No introduction is necessary! Why, this has to be the incredible woman that has changed Tim's life, Karen.

JODY:   [to Tim] What?!

DAVE:   It is so nice to . . . meet . . .wait, I am confused. Jennifer . . . [begins to scramble] ah, Nancy? Betty? . . .

JODY:   [to Tim, angry] Why, you no good, two-faced, lying cheat! Don't you ever call me or talk to me again.

[Jody exits.]

DAVE:   [still trying to connect] Mary? No, she has to be Sandy!

TIM:    [defeated] Dave! Put a sock in it. She's gone.

DAVE:   [genuinely sorry] Hey pal, sorry. I guess I blew your cover, huh?

TIM:    Big time. Oh well, better luck next time.

DAVE:   Yeah, no problem; plenty of fish in the sea.

[freeze; blackout]

# SCENE 2

*Jody and Angie are stage left, finding their seats in the movie theater, holding their popcorn and sodas. At the same time, Dave and Tim are walking into their apartment. When one person is speaking the other duo freezes. It works best to have the duos interchange rapidly.*

JODY:    *[angry]* Men! Angie, let me tell you all men are liars and cheats. You can't believe a thing they say. *[freeze]*

TIM:    Women! The minute you say something nice, they expect the world. And then, when they don't get what they want, they blow up in your face. You can't win for losing! *[freeze]*

ANGIE:    Losers! They are all a bunch of losers. I can't believe how immature men are. And why do they have to lie? *[freeze]*

DAVE:    Lies! They accuse us of lying. It's not lying, Tim. Believe me, we're just telling them what they want to hear. *[freeze]*

JODY:    Hear me out, Angie. I am declaring a moratorium on men. I have had it. It is the single life for me. You can't trust one of them, and you know I am not exaggerating! *[freeze]*

TIM:    Exaggeration! All they do is exaggerate. It is "you always" or "you never" or "all men are alike." Dave, that is just as big a lie as any. Not all men are like us, why some are— *[freeze]*

ANGIE:    Honest! Just give me an honest man, and I will have him encased in bronze. That is a— *[freeze]*

DAVE:    Promises! That's what they want! Ridiculous, unrealistic promises. No one could keep the promises they want us to keep.

*[Tim gets up to turn on the TV; freeze]*

VOICE-OVER #1:    *[to women]* We are sorry to inform you that due to technical difficulties we will not be able to show the movie as scheduled. Refunds for tickets will be at the counter on your way out. *[freeze]*

TIM:    All right. Go Broncos!

VOICE-OVER #2:    We regret to inform you that due to a management error the game of the week will not be shown. Stayed tuned for a special program.

ALL FOUR
CHARACTERS:    See, you just can't believe anyone!

*[freeze; blackout]*

## 8

*Too Late*

## THEME

Jesus is coming again. Some take it seriously, and others don't. Some are ready, and others are not. Some will be taken, and others, as in this sketch, will be left behind.

## CHARACTERS

WILBUR:  Sixty-five years old and has a harried personality. His clothes don't match, and he carries binoculars, a small suitcase, and wears a special hat.

WENDEL:  Wilbur's redneck neighbor. He is close to Wilbur's age. He is dressed in a flannel shirt, blue jeans, and suspenders.

EMILY:  A senior saint and not all of her "ducks are in a row." She is a bit eccentric in her dress, and she carries a large purse.

ESTHER:  A "church lady," religious to the core. She is younger than Emily and a perfect match to Emily in dress.

LUANN:  Esther's teenage daughter, a chip off the old block.

VOICE-OVER:  Authoritative voice, reading Scripture.

## SETTING

Scene 1:  An open stage.
Scene 2:  A church with two rows of chairs or pews.

## SCENE 1

*Fast-paced music begins. The theme to* Mission Impossible *would be ideal. Wilbur enters, races around the platform, sets down a small suitcase, and uses binoculars to look up into the ceiling. It is obvious he is frantically looking for something in the sky. Wendel enters and watches Wilbur for a moment.*

WENDEL:  *[loudly]* Wilbur! Wilbur! What are you doing?

WILBUR:  *[stops for just a second to see who is yelling at him, but keeps looking up through his binoculars]* Oh, hi, Wendel. Just looking.

WENDEL:  No kidding. Looking for what?

WILBUR:  Didn't you hear Pastor _____ *[fill in name of your pastor]* last week?

WENDEL:  No, I didn't. You know I'm not into that church-going stuff. Going to church doesn't make someone a Christian any more than going into a garage makes someone a car. So now what is it that the Reverend was talking about?

WILBUR:   Well, he said Jesus is coming again, in the clouds, and it could be any day. I . . . I don't want to miss it.

WENDEL:   You're missing your marbles is what you're missing. Come on, Wilbur, you don't really believe that stuff?

WILBUR:   Go ahead, Wendel, make fun of me all you want. But I believe the Bible, and when it happens, I'm going to be ready. Besides, I've got my favorite hat. I'm ready to go.

WENDEL:   You're going to need more than your hat, pal. I can't believe this guy, starts going to church, prays a few prayers, gives his life to God, and now he's going off the deep end. Whatever happened to good ol' common sense? Good grief.

*[Music resumes. Wendel exits back stage. Wilbur keeps looking up as he exits up center aisle.]*

## SCENE 2

*Organ music plays an old-fashioned hymn like "Sweet Hour of Prayer" or "Bringing in the Sheaves." Three ladies enter and find their seats in church.*

EMILY:   Hello, Esther. *[yawns]*

ESTHER:   Emily . . . did you get that honey muffin recipe I sent you?

EMILY:   Yep . . . didn't work. You forgot the eggs.

ESTHER:   I did not forget the eggs. You probably forgot to put them in.

EMILY:   *[pulls out recipe card from her purse]* You forgot the eggs.

ESTHER:   Always have to be right, don't you, Emily? Can never be wrong. *[looking around]* So, answer lady, where is everybody? It is almost time for church to start.

LuANN:   I told you we didn't have to come this early, Mother.

ESTHER:   *[looking around, past LuAnn]* Did I hear something? *[to Emily]* You know, children are to be seen, not heard.

EMILY:   Especially in church.

ESTHER:   Well, we finally agree on something.

EMILY:   *[looking at watch, becoming a bit nervous]* Reverend _____ is never late. *[getting excited]* Do you think? Could it possibly be . . .

| ESTHER/EMILY: | *[in unison]* The week of the time change. *[Both begin to pat their brow in relief.]* |
|---|---|
| LUANN: | Ah, Mother . . . |
| ESTHER: | Oh, Emily, my dear, I am so relieved. |
| EMILY: | Me too. You know, for a moment, for just a split second, I thought— |
| ESTHER: | Thought it was that "rupture" thing that the Reverend was talking about last week. You know, when all of us good saints go straight up in that there smoke cloud when it comes. |
| LUANN: | Mother, the time change was three weeks ago. |
| ESTHER: | Oh, another answer lady. Then how do you explain why everyone is not here today? |
| LUANN: | I don't know, ask Miss Emily. |
| EMILY: | Time change, kid. Maybe they are doing an extra one this year, and we missed the announcement. Let me check my calendar. Maybe we got the wrong date. You know, my brother Wilbur said he was going to be at church today. I wonder where he is? |
| ESTHER: | Wilbur? You know you can't depend on him. Always late. Why, he'd miss the Good Lord's return if it wasn't for some angel blowing a trumpet. |

*[Wendel enters, carrying Wilbur's hat and binoculars.]*

| EMILY: | Well, hold on to your pew, look who is in church. Hang on to your hat, Esther, the roof may cave in. |
|---|---|
| WENDEL: | Hello, Miss Emily, Esther . . . |
| ESTHER: | This isn't Easter or Christmas, Wendel. What are you doing here, and what is with the hat and spyglasses? |
| WENDEL: | *[nervous and humble]* I'm not sure. This is Wilbur's hat, and I found it in his driveway today, next to these. *[holds out binoculars]* I can't find Wilbur anywhere. He's gone, just gone. I knocked on his door. I mean, Wilbur is always home on Sunday morning, at least until he goes to church, so I thought that maybe I could find him here. *[to himself]* He kept talking about Jesus coming again, and I remember hearing about that stuff when I was a kid— |
| EMILY: | Wendel, don't you fret one bit. If that trumpet would have blown Esther and me would have been the first to go. Yes, sir. We are the pillars around |

this place. [points forward] See those drapes up there? I made those. Esther, tell him what you did.

ESTHER:    I waxed the floor in the foyer this week.

EMILY:    Go on, don't hold back, dear!

ESTHER:    Well, I cleaned the oven in the church kitchen, too.

EMILY:    There you have it. No trumpet, no Rapture. Reverend _____ is just plain late, and it is a time-change Sunday.

WENDEL:    No, the time change was three weeks ago.

LuANN:    I told you it wasn't the time change.

EMILY/ESTHER:    [panic/in unison] Give me those glasses.

[They both grab the binoculars and look up in the ceiling, one on each half. The others on stage also look up and freeze.]

VOICE-OVER:    "For the Lord himself will come down from heaven, with the trumpet call of God and we who are still alive will be caught up with him in the clouds, to meet the Lord. And this day will come in a moment that no one knows, it will come in a twinkling of an eye, like a thief in the night."

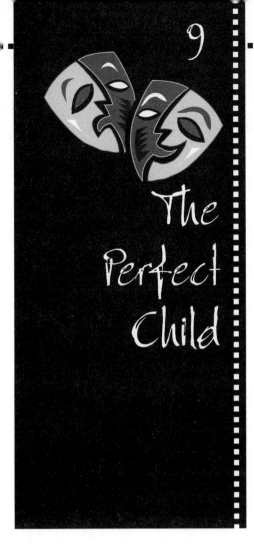

## 9

# The Perfect Child

## THEME

God says, "Be holy, for I am holy." We do not always understand what holiness is all about. We have our own definition that is often connected with being perfect and trying to impress God with our righteousness. This sketch is a bit of a spoof on a couple who try to be perfect parents. They set out to do all the right things, until the first problem causes them to see imperfection.

## CHARACTERS

WENDELL:  The perfect husband who thinks of everything. He is in his twenties or thirties, dressed casually.

MARGARET:  Wendell's perfect wife who does everything just right. She is also dressed casually.

## SETTING

Scene 1:  Set with a small table with linen, candles, and a few pieces of china.
Scene 2:  Set with a crib or bassinet.

## SCENE 1

*Soft music sets the stage. Wendell and Margaret come to the table.
Wendell helps Margaret with her chair. They are very formal and polite
to each other.*

WENDELL:  Well, my dear Margaret, what brings about the honor and delight of this special occasion?

MARGARET:  *[almost shy]* Oh, Wendell, we have waited for this moment for a long time. Our first will soon arrive.

WENDELL:  Darling! Is it? Could it be? Are we really . . .

TOGETHER:  Pregnant!

MARGARET:  *[cheesy]* Oh, Wendell, I am so excited, are you?

WENDELL:  Of course, my dear. Whatever else could I be?

MARGARET:  We have planned and prepared and now here we are!

41

WENDELL:    Yes, indeed. . . . Now, we need to rehearse the things we have learned. *[He stands as if making a speech.]* Certainly, we are going to be perfect parents with a perfect child. There is no other option.

MARGARET:    *[joins in the speech]* We don't have a thing to worry about, sweetheart. Why, with my degree in childhood education . . .

WENDELL:    And the degree I have earned in adolescent psychology . . .

MARGARET:    Just for this child!

TOGETHER:    We can't lose.

WENDELL:    Another Nobel Prize winner.

MARGARET:    No doubt a senator.

WENDELL:    *[businesslike]* Do you have the route laid out to get to the hospital?

MARGARET:    Certainly, and the Hooked-on-Phonics course is ordered.

WENDELL:    Military school applications are all set?

MARGARET:    And I called the *Who's Who in America* committee as well as the National Honors Society in advance, of course.

WENDELL:    All medications, vaccinations, and examinations will be ordered tomorrow.

MARGARET:    I need your signature on the summer camp program and an advance deposit for violin lessons.

WENDELL:    Very good, and you will need to set up the schedule for an exchange student program and driver's training.

MARGARET:    *[with wonder and joy]* Wendell, this child is going to be . . . famous.

*[They both put clothes pins on noses.]*

WENDELL:    *[reaches into coat and pulls out a can of Lysol]* Deodorizer!

MARGARET:    *[reaches into purse and pulls out a liquid cleaner bottle]* Disinfectant!

TOGETHER:    Let's have this baby!

*[freeze; blackout]*

## SCENE 2

*Margaret and Wendell enter singing or humming a lullaby as they carry a baby (doll) all wrapped up in a blanket. Just before Margaret lays the infant down in the crib, Wendell sprays everything with his can of deodorizer/disinfectant.*

MARGARET: *[with great tenderness]* He is looking at you, dear.

WENDELL: *[melodramatic]* He has your eyes.

MARGARET: And your . . . chins . . .

WENDELL: *[not too sure, but kindly]* Ah, yes . . . he is simply . . .

TOGETHER: Perfect.

MARGARET: *[excited]* Remarkable.

WENDELL: *[proud]* A genius.

MARGARET: Dear? Shall we begin?

WENDELL: *[reaches in pocket and pulls out two pencils]* Son! How many pencils do I have in my hand? *[expectant pause]*

MARGARET: *[serious]* Maybe he didn't hear you, or maybe he was distracted. Yes, that's it . . . try again, dear.

WENDELL: No, he heard me. The question was far too simple. That is the reason for no response. *[leans in holding pencils]* Son, if Daddy paid twenty-five cents for one pencil and twenty cents for the other, and if he gave the clerk a one dollar bill, with 6.5 percent sales tax added to the transaction, how much change would Daddy receive? *[Both look intently for a response.]*

MARGARET: I think he is tired from the hospital, dear. We can try again later.

WENDELL: I am sure you are correct, dear. These little minds need lots of rest. Son, we will work on vowels in the morning.

MARGARET: *[sniffing]* Wendell, did you deodorize the nursery?

WENDELL: Of course I did.

MARGARET: *[sniffing in the air]* Then what on earth is that odor?

WENDELL: I don't know. . . . *[sniffing]* It is certainly nothing I have ever noticed before.

MARGARET: *[looks around]* You did secure all of the windows and doors?

WENDELL: And the heat ducts have triple air water filters.

MARGARET: *[looks at baby]* You don't think . . .

WENDELL: *[confident]* Not a chance.

MARGARET: *[concerned]* But it might be.

WENDELL: *[questionable]* But how could our son ever—

MARGARET: *[close to baby, panicking]* Wendell, our son—

TOGETHER: Is not perfect!

MARGARET: *[panics]* What are we going to do?

WENDELL: *[out of control]* Call 911, the hospital, get an ambulance!

MARGARET: Wendell, we have failed.

WENDELL: There is no hope.

MARGARET: What will become of him?

WENDELL: Maybe he will become—

TOGETHER: *[shriek]* NORMAL!

*[freeze; blackout]*

## THEME

Sexual addictions usually begin on a very small scale. Pornography often leads to action as the fantasy becomes reality. This sketch reveals the devastating long-term effects of pornography as well as the apparently subtle beginnings.

## CHARACTERS

TOMMY:  About eleven years old. He is dressed casually and carries a ball glove, a ball, and some baseball cards.

JOEY:  Tommy's good friend, a couple of years older and much "wiser." He is dressed casually, wears a ball glove, and carries a magazine with the word "Girls" taped to the front.

## SETTING

Only a simple set is required for the two boys to be able to sit and dialogue. A bench would work just fine, or even the front edge of the stage.

*Tommy and Joey play catch with a ball as they dialogue.*

JOEY:    Hey, Tommy, what do you think of Jennifer?

TOMMY:   She's too tall. Did you go to the last _____ *[name of local or state baseball team]* game?

JOEY:    *[not interested]* Nope. . . . Hey, how about Melissa? She is so cool, and she is good in math.

TOMMY:   Joey, she is too old. What did you think of _____ *[baseball pitcher]* pitching last week?

JOEY:    *[as if he never heard Tommy's question]* Samantha, whoa, did you see the way she moves?

TOMMY:   *[factually]* Yeah, what's wrong with her?

JOEY:    Tommy, what is your problem? These are the greatest "women" God created, and they are a-vail-a-ble.

TOMMY:   For what? They can't hit worth beans. And have you seen the way they throw? *[mimics action]* Look, someday I'm going to play professional baseball, so girls can wait.

JOEY:      You just don't get it, do you, moron? You are such a nerd.

TOMMY:    Just 'cause you're girl crazy.

JOEY:      Hey, just 'cause you're a dumb kid. You're into home runs, and I'm into hormones.

TOMMY:    What's that?

JOEY:      Boy, are you out of it. Don't you know nothing?

TOMMY:    *[pause]* Hey, want to see my latest baseball cards?

JOEY:      *[being polite]* Sure. *[They sit down on a bench or on the front edge of the stage.]* And when you're done, I've got something to show you.

TOMMY:    What's that?

JOEY:      You'll see.

TOMMY:    Okay, but I've got to be home early to take a bath, 'cause it's Saturday night. *[pulls cards out of his pocket and holds a card up]* Can you believe _____? *[baseball star]* His batting average is the best in the league.

JOEY:      Is not.

TOMMY:    Is too.

JOEY:      Who cares?

TOMMY:    *[holding up another card]* I just love the way that _____ *[baseball star]* plays third base. He never misses the ball. He's just great, huh, Joey?

JOEY:      Yeah, Tommy great . . . real great. *[looking around to see if anyone is watching them]* But trust me, you have not seen great yet.

TOMMY:    Here it is, Joey. This is my Rookie of the Year card. It's worth about a million dollars. I wouldn't trade it for anything.

JOEY:      A million bucks? Come on, it's worth about six bucks. And I'll tell you what I would trade it for—*[reaches for his back pocket and pulls out a magazine that says "Girls" on the front]* this! Look at that, Tommy.

*[Joey thrusts the now open magazine into Tommy's face. Tommy is shocked and speechless for a moment.]*

TOMMY: *[nervous and appears distressed]* Joey! Is that . . . is that . . . phone-augraphy?

JOEY: What? Tommy, that is the most gorgeous babe in the whole world.

TOMMY: *[looking around to be sure no one sees them]* But, Joey, she doesn't have any . . . she is all . . .

JOEY: Yeah, isn't it great?

TOMMY: I don't know, Joey. I don't think we should be looking at this. Where did you get that anyway?

JOEY: Hey, my dad won't miss it. He has tons of them.

TOMMY: Well, I don't think it is . . . right. We shouldn't be looking at this stuff, and what if your mom or dad catches us?

JOEY: *[cool and calm]* Hey, no big deal. I got caught once already, and I just got this weird lecture that didn't make any sense at all. So, relax man . . . and enjoy it!

TOMMY: *[nervous]* I think I better go now.

JOEY: Come on, Tommy, be honest. Don't you think this is the best thing you ever saw? *[shoves magazine back in Tommy's face]*

TOMMY: *[shows some signs of weakness]* Well, yeah . . . sort of . . . kind of. It's okay, I guess.

JOEY: You guess? I guess so! This will change your life. This stuff will make you a real man, Tommy.

TOMMY: *[saddened]* It didn't help my dad. That's why he's not home anymore.

JOEY: What do you mean?

TOMMY: Mom says that Dad left because he got in a lot of trouble and had to go away for therapy, and it all started with phone-augraphy.

JOEY: Come on, what can this hurt? Look, it's just a bunch of pictures. No big deal.

TOMMY: It hurt my mom a lot, Joey. And to me, it is a big deal, 'cause now I don't have a dad who will look at my baseball cards. *[looks at Joey with magazine and stands up]* And I guess I don't have a friend who wants to look at my cards either. *[starts to leave]* See ya, Joey.

JOEY:    *[a bit stunned]* Wait a minute, Tommy. I don't have to look at this anymore. *[Tommy turns, looks at Joey with disapproval, and walks on.]* Besides, they are just pictures. *[Drops magazine and runs to catch up to Tommy.]*

*[freeze; blackout]*

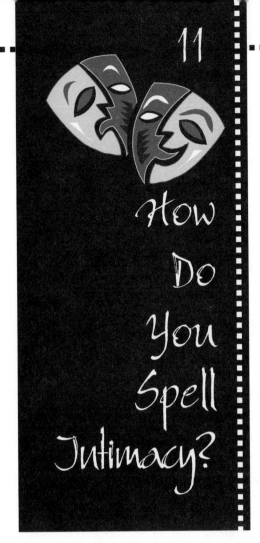

**11**

## How Do You Spell Intimacy?

## THEME

Intimacy is often spelled s-e-x. It is no different in this sketch . . . or is it? A sexual encounter may be a critical part of an intimate relationship, but God's design for intimacy goes much further than that.

## CHARACTERS

MARLA: She is having an affair and thinks she deserves it. After all, she's a modern woman. She is dressed semi-casually.

VIRGINIA: She is not having an affair but wishes she was. She is a bit naive and even a bit jealous of Marla's new love. She is dressed semi-casually.

ROXANNE: She is the stereotypical gum-chewing waitress at the local diner. She has wisdom that our other two friends seem to lack. She wears a waitress uniform.

## SETTING

Scene 1: Two telephones at each end of the stage.
Scene 2: The set is a simple café table with white or checkered table-cloth, flowers, and a few dish items. Menus are used.

## SCENE 1

*Marla and Virginia are standing on opposite ends of the platform. Each is holding a telephone. They begin in a freeze position and become animated as Marla begins the dialogue.*

MARLA: *[very excited]* Virginia, I just have to meet you for lunch.

VIRGINIA: *[responds just as excited]* Wow, sounds important. Marla, you won the Lotto!

MARLA: Oh, I wish, but this is even better.

VIRGINIA: I can't imagine what would be better than winning three million dollars. So, this better be good.

MARLA: It is better than good, it's great!

VIRGINIA: How about meeting at the Bistro?

MARLA: No, too many people know me there. Big ears around that place.

VIRGINIA: Well, how about that little urban café on 34th Street.

MARLA:    That's fine. See you *[looks at watch]* in twenty minutes. Ta, ta!

VIRGINIA:    Twenty minutes nothing! I will be there in five. *[hangs up phone, speaking to herself]* Oh, Marla, I think you have gone too far this time. *[to audience]* And I can just imagine what you are thinking.

## SCENE 2

*Marla and Virginia approach the table. They are acting rather silly and a bit giddy.*

VIRGINIA:    Marla, tell me, what is the big news?

MARLA:    Virginia, I think I'm in love!

VIRGINIA:    Well, of course you are, or at least you should be. You and Barry have been married . . . six years now?

*[Roxanne enters and gives them menus.]*

ROXANNE:    I'll be back with some ice water. Anything else I can bring you to drink?

BOTH:    *[ignoring Roxanne]* No, thanks . . .

ROXANNE:    I love this job.

MARLA:    Virginia, it's not Barry. His name is David.

VIRGINIA:    David? Marla, ah, I can't believe you. Why, it is so unlike—

MARLA:    Unlike me? You will never know until you try it, dear. *[sitting back, relaxed]* You know, these things just . . . happen.

VIRGINIA:    *[disturbed]* But I thought that you and—

MARLA:    Barry? Honey, you don't know Barry like I know Barry.

VIRGINIA:    But he is so gorgeous, your man is such a—

MARLA:    Slob! A good-looking slob. The only thing he takes care of is himself with a capital H.

VIRGINIA:    Ooooo, I didn't realize that things were that—

MARLA:    Tense? Real tense! Virginia, from the first day back from the honeymoon, that ego-centered King of Slobbovia has carpeted the floor with his hair and sprayed the walls with the worst aftershave known to man and beast. Why, his idea of taking out the trash is driving his car to work. He never talks to me, unless it is about his stuff. *[forlorn]* He never holds my hand anymore. The compliments disappeared along with dinner dates, which were replaced by the remote control and the sports section of the newspaper.

ROXANNE:     *[walks into conversation]* Okay, ladies, what will it be?

VIRGINIA:     *[scrambles for menu]* Oh, I'll have the diet plate.

MARLA:     I'll have the barbecue sandwich.

ROXANNE:     *[yells back to the kitchen]* One fruit cup and a Sloppy Joe!

BOTH:     Sounds like my husband.

VIRGINIA:     *[looks around]* Marla, well, tell me about . . . David.

MARLA:     Wonderful, Virginia. He is Mr. Wonderful. He talks to me. He is happy just to hold my hand over the lunch hour. And he has no idea where the sports section is. And the best news, he doesn't make those disgusting noises at the table.

VIRGINIA:     Life is so unfair. Why couldn't . . . God bring us Mr. Wonderful the first time? Why did we have to get stuck with good old rent-a-wreck? *[switches gears]* Oh, Marla, you are so lucky. Tell me more about you and David.

MARLA:     Well, he sends me notes that say the kindest things . . . and just the way he looks at me! The last time I saw Barry look that way was at a pizza, with tomato sauce running down his forearm.

VIRGINIA:     Oh, it sounds so intimate. *[leveling]* Now, tell me the truth. Have you and David? . . . You know, have you two . . .

MARLA:     Slept together? Virginia, what do you think? I have never been happier in my life. How else do you spell intimacy?

ROXANNE:     *[walks into conversation again, to Virginia]* One diet plate for you *[to Marla]* and one affair for you.

MARLA:     *[look of shock and embarrassment]* Ahh, excuse me? How did you? *[totally flustered]*

ROXANNE:     *[to the point]* Look, I wasn't born yesterday. I see it in here all the time.

VIRGINIA:     *[defensive]* Well, I think it is wonderful.

ROXANNE: Look, ladies, let me give you a tip, and this one is on me. I'll agree, the grass does look greener, but it is going to need cutting and watering just like every other yard in the neighborhood. And remember, you can't make anything grow by yourself, but you can do a whole lot to kill the yard you have. Trust me, ladies, I know what I am talking about, and your better days are not ahead of you. Go ahead, keep messing around, keep dreaming, but intimacy is not a three-letter word. Well, have a nice day. *[exits]*

VIRGINIA: Why, of all the nerve.

MARLA: *[rather somber]* No, Virginia, what if she is right?

VIRGINIA: *[still defensive]* And what if she is? Barry is still a slob, and David is your knight in shining armor.

MARLA: You're right on both counts, but my slob is my slob, and as for knights in shining armor, I think they're found only in fairy tales. *[gets up from her seat]* Excuse me, Virginia. I think I need to go home and . . . mow the grass.

*[freeze; blackout]*

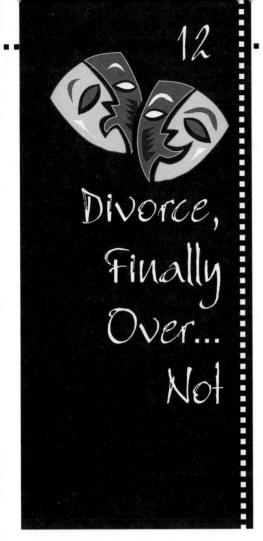

## THEME

Most people actually believe that when the gavel falls on a divorce decree, it is all over. Quite the contrary, new problems have just begun. The ongoing financial, custody, and daily battles seem to never end. This sketch reminds us of the ongoing struggle, pain, and hurt that come from divorce. Remember, God said, "I hate divorce."

## CHARACTERS

BETH: She has just gone through a divorce and is in obvious pain and shock. She is dressed in nice slacks and top.

TERRY: Beth's new neighbor. She has all the answers as she tries to console her new friend. She is dressed very casually.

JILL: Beth's teenage daughter. She is angry about her parents' divorce. Today, she is blaming her mom for all that has happened. She is dressed as a typical teen.

JIMMY: Beth's youngest child. He loves his mom and dad, and he feels responsible for his parents' divorce. He is dressed in play clothes.

## SETTING

Scene 1: At stage right, two institutional tables create a laundry room folding area in an apartment building.

Scene 2: At stage left, a card table, three chairs, cereal boxes, bowls, and donuts create a kitchen for breakfast time. A boom box and a telephone are needed as props.

## SCENE 1

*Terry is first on the scene, dumping all of her laundry on the table to fold it. She is whistling and having a good time. Beth comes in later with her laundry, looking exhausted.*

TERRY: *[gregarious]* Hi, I'm Terry.

BETH: *[tired]* Good morning.

TERRY: Good morning? Whoa, you must be new around here.

BETH: My kids and I moved in here on Monday. How many quarters does it take to get the towels dry?

TERRY: Let me guess. You are just divorced. This is not your side of town. Your ex is a real jerk. You don't want to be here. And the towels never really get dry. How am I doing?

BETH: *[a small smile]* I think you're psychic.

53

TERRY:    Nope, I've just seen a lot of them come through looking just like you. Your manicure and . . . your frown gave you away. So, let me start over for both of us. Hi, I'm Terry, Terry Cook. How about you?

BETH:    Beth, Beth Daniels. We are in 215 upstairs.

TERRY:    Well, listen, you will get used to this dump. It kind of grows on you after a while.

BETH:    *[looking around]* I suppose that is something to look forward to.

TERRY:    Just watch out for the super. He doesn't tolerate slamming doors after midnight, and loud music is a big no-no before he has had his coffee at seven in the morning. Other than that, you will be on easy street.

BETH:    *[looks around again]* Easy street? This wasn't quite what I had in mind. But this is only temporary.

TERRY:    Yep, been temporary for me, too—about twelve years of temporary. I bet you lived in a big place out in the burbs?

BETH:    Five bedrooms and four baths.

TERRY:    Sweetie, you didn't lose anything. Who would want to clean all those bathrooms?

BETH:    Well, I didn't have to . . .

TERRY:    A maid? No kidding! You had a maid? I have never met someone who had a maid.

BETH:    *[a bit apologetic]* She just came in two days a week.

TERRY:    So, are you working?

BETH:    *[picking up a piece of laundry]* What do you call this?

TERRY:    No, a job. Like in paycheck? Punch the clock?

BETH:    I started looking yesterday in the newspaper. The support check I get from Roger is not going to cut it, and my attorney wants his money. And . . . I just don't have the skills employers are demanding.

TERRY:    Sure you do. The way you fold that towel, you could get a job down at Z-marts. I heard they are hiring sales clerks and . . . associates. Jobs start around _____ *[fill in average dollar amount]* an hour. *[finishes up her laundry and picks up her basket]* If you need anything, I'm right above you in 315. Hey, you're going to make it. *[very sympathetic]* I did, and I know what you are going through.

BETH: Thanks . . . thanks, Terry. Nice meeting you. *[Terry exits.]* $_____ *[above amount]* an hour? Roger, I hope you are satisfied. *[slams the remainder of her clothes into the basket]* And I hope that you and that little girlfriend of yours have the most . . . miserable life anyone could ever have.

*[freeze; blackout]*

## SCENE 2

*Jill is eating a donut and listening to her boom box, which is cranked up very loudly. Jimmy is just sitting, stirring his cereal with no expression. Beth comes walking in with her laundry basket as the phone begins to ring.*

BETH: *[to Jill]* Honey, would you please turn your radio down? *[picks up the phone]* Hello, hello? I'm sorry, I didn't hear you. . . . Yes, this is Beth Daniels. *[listens]* $300 for the transmission? But I don't have . . . Can I pay you later? *[pause]* I see, you need the money before I can get the car back. Yes, thank you. *[hangs up phone and yells with frustration]* Jill, would you turn that music down? How many times have I told you to turn that stuff down when I am on the phone? You don't have to play it at full blast! And it's not even 7 A.M., and the building superintendent is probably going to call and complain about the noise.

JILL: *[smart mouth]* The only thing anyone can hear around here is your yelling.

BETH: You watch your mouth, young lady.

JILL: *[turns music off in anger]* There *[click]* are you satisfied? Is everything just perfect now?

BETH: Jill, honey, I need your help, not your grief.

JILL: *[sarcastic]* Then why do we have stale donuts ev-er-y day for breakfast, and cereal without milk?

BETH: Honey, I am doing the best I can. You know how much money your father sends us. . . . There is just not enough to pay the bills.

JILL: *[raising voice]* But you can buy a new dress, and we can't have milk.

BETH: That is the first dress I have bought this year, and I need it for job interviews.

JIMMY: *[upset]* Would you guys stop yelling?

BETH: *[yelling]* We are not yelling, Jimmy. . . . *[calmly]* We are discussing.

JILL: Sure, Mom, another one of your discussions that always end with whatever you say.

BETH: Jill, what is the problem?

JILL: You, Mom. You're the problem. *[getting up]* Dad would never have left if it hadn't been for your complaining and nagging him all the time. *[leaving]* This is all your fault.

BETH: Where are you going?

JILL: I'll be back when you see me.

*[Beth sits down next to Jimmy, discouraged.]*

JIMMY: Mom?

BETH: Yes, Jimmy.

JIMMY: The divorce wasn't your fault, Mom.

BETH: *[tender]* You're a sweet boy, Jimmy, nothing like your . . .

JIMMY: Mom, I think the divorce was my fault.

BETH: Why do you say that?

JIMMY: Well, if I hadn't been naughty that one time, then you and Dad wouldn't have yelled at each other. And if you hadn't yelled, then you wouldn't have gotten a divorce.

BETH: Oh, Jimmy, this is not your fault.

JIMMY: Mom, will God leave us like Dad did?

BETH: I hope not, Son. I hope not.

JIMMY: I hope He doesn't either. I think we really need God, don't you, Mom?

BETH: Yes, honey, yes we do.

JIMMY: Mom, don't you worry about anything, because I can eat cereal without milk for a long time.

*[freeze; blackout]*

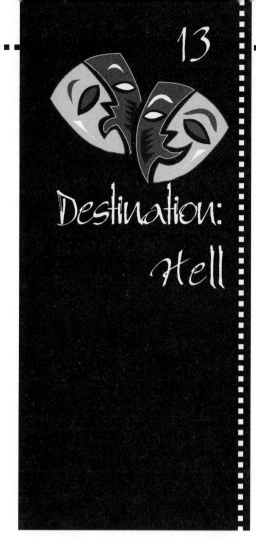

## 13

Destination: Hell

## THEME

We don't like to talk about hell. So, we don't. This sketch brings out a few of the biblical ideas about the place of eternal separation from God. In scene 1, our character is given all the lies needed to stay on his pathway toward eternal destruction. Scene 2 is a hard lesson in reality.

## CHARACTERS

LEONARD WALKER:  A rather gullible and naive tourist. He first calls, then goes to the travel agency dressed in a flowered shirt, Bermuda shorts, black kneesocks, and straw hat, with a camera around his neck.

AGENT D'CEIVER:  A rather demonic sort of character. His devilish laugh and sly manner mark him as a conniving sort of fellow. He can be dressed in a suit. A bright red tie or red shirt would be excellent.

## SETTING

At stage left is a door with side panels. A smoke machine would be ideal behind the door. A sign on the door reads 7734 (upside down, it reads hell). Just in front of the door, off to the side, is a small desk, a phone, and two chairs with a sign, "Eternal Vacations," hanging on the front of the desk. At stage right, another chair, end table, and phone represents Leonard's living room.

*Leonard is sitting in his living room reading a brochure.*

LEONARD: Wow, does this look like a great vacation! Boy, that is just what I need. Let me see . . . *[reads brochure]* Eternal Vacations offers the best in getaways. Get away from all of your hassles and worries. Get away from all of the annoying problems of everyday life. Get away with us by calling 666-1666. Hmmmmm. That is for me and the missus. *[reaches over to dial phone . . . phone rings in Agent's office]* Eternal Vacations, it sounds just heavenly.

*[Agent enters stage left through the smoke filled door, coughing and wheezing and grumbling.]*

AGENT: I've got to do something about all of this smoke, not real good for business. *[grumbling to the phone, still ringing]* Yeah, yeah, I'm coming. . . . You don't have to be in such a big hurry. *[total change in voice, kind yet sly]* Eternal Vacations . . . Agent D'Ceiver here. How can I help you?

LEONARD: Hi, Mr. D'Ceiver, this is Leonard Walker. I was just reading your ad for an Eternal Vacation. It sounds like the perfect getaway. Do you still have some vacancies?

AGENT: Leonard, my friend, we have plenty of room for you and the missus.

LEONARD: Hey, that sounds great! *[puzzled]* By the way, how did you know that I am married?

AGENT: Oh, let's just say we are well networked, and we know more than you think.

LEONARD: Well, okay. . . . Now, do you have a place that is warm?

AGENT: Warmth is no problem at our Eternal Vacations spots.

LEONARD: Just get me out of this cold.

AGENT: No problem, Leonard, no problem.

LEONARD: Great. Now, I want a real getaway. You know, no phones, no pesky neighbors, and no door-to-door salesmen.

AGENT: Leonard, we guarantee that no one will knock on your door.

LEONARD: Well, that sounds terrific. Can I bring the kids?

AGENT: Leonard, you can bring anyone you want. We don't turn anyone away.

LEONARD: This is great! You folks sure are accommodating.

AGENT: We are here to make you happy, Leonard. Happy, happy, happy!

LEONARD: Just tell me what to do to register.

AGENT: Leonard, you are all set. Your name is in our reservation file. You have nothing more to do other than come and enjoy your Eternal Vacation.

LEONARD: Already registered? . . . This is too good to be true.

AGENT: It couldn't be truer, Leonard. Just come on down to the agency and pick up your tickets. They are waiting for you. Your reservation number is 7734.

LEONARD: Wait, let me get that number again. Vacation package number 7-7-3-4. Thank you, and I'll be down as soon as I can.

*[freeze; blackout]*

*Director's Note: The character can move directly from his living room to the agent's office, or take a break between the two scenes.*

## SCENE 2

*Leonard walks from stage right, his living room, to stage left, the agent's office. He approaches the Eternal Vacations desk and knocks or rings a bell, if available.*

LEONARD:  *[still excited]* Hello, hello, is anybody here?

AGENT:  *[comes walking out of smoke-filled doorway, coughing]* Leonard, Leonard, we have been expecting you. How can I help you?

LEONARD:  Wow, you already know my name. You guys are really sharp. Well, I'm here to get my tickets for *[looks at card]* vacation package number 7734. Hey, that's my number right there on your door.

AGENT:  Leonard, that is our most popular package. Absolutely guaranteed.

LEONARD:  Boy, this is getting better and better all the time. By the way, the missus wanted me to ask you who has gone on this trip before. We would like to check with some former travelers—you know, what to wear, what to bring, that sort of thing.

AGENT:  Leonard, most everyone in your community has either taken our vacation package or they are registered for a future trip. You have nothing to worry about. Our trip is very popular. And you don't need to worry about bringing anything. We furnish all that you will ever need. Trust me, Leonard.

LEONARD:  This is unbelievable. Now, how do I pay for the tickets?

AGENT:  We'll charge it to your account. And the best news is, Leonard, that you pay after you take your trip. Nothing more is needed up front. You are all set and ready to go. Just follow me.

*[Agent opens door for Leonard, who goes through, and shuts the door. Agent stands by door amused and laughing. Lights go out in auditorium.]*

LEONARD:  *[offstage, loudly, almost yelling]* Hey, it sure is dark in here. Could someone turn on the lights or at least the air conditioner? It must be 110 degrees in here. And, by the way, I requested the no smoking section. This place *[coughs]* is terrible. And how come I am all alone in here? I wanted a getaway, but this is ridiculous. I didn't mean isolation. Could somebody tell me where I am?

*[Spotlight comes up on door. Agent turns sign upside down, reading hell.]*

LEONARD:  Hey, Mr. D'Ceiver . . . I don't think this is what I had in mind. I would like a refund, please.

AGENT:  There are no refunds, Leonard. *[to the audience]* There are no refunds.

*[music; freeze; blackout]*

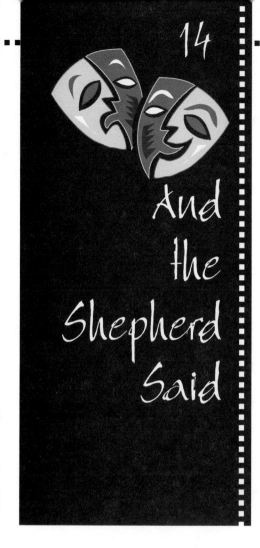

## 14

# And the Shepherd Said

## THEME

The true meaning of Christmas is lost in the busyness and materialism of our culture. A simple manger scene and a "talking shepherd" reminds us of who we should be focusing our attention on during the Christmas—and every—season.

## CHARACTERS

MR. DIRECTOR: A flamboyant Christmas program director, hurrying to his performance. He hurries right past the manger scene, oblivious to the Christmas story. He is dressed in bright holiday colors.

MRS. SHOPALL: A fast-moving character who is on a mission with her shopping bag and list. She is annoyed by the shepherd who is trying to get her attention. She is dressed in an overcoat and mittens.

TWO TEENAGE GIRLS: They are caught up in conversation about everything but the Christmas story. Their dress reflects the most contemporary styles.

BUSINESSMAN: A fast-moving business executive with cell phone, top coat, and hat.

YOUNG MAN: Rather quiet and forlorn. He is the only one who listens to the shepherd. His dress is casual.

SHEPHERD: The talking shepherd is a voice offstage.

STAGEHAND: Dressed in overalls and flannel shirt and wears a headset/radio. He carries the manger scene out to center stage.

## SETTING

A tabletop manger scene (crèche) is placed by the stagehand at stage center on a small pedestal. A park bench is alongside the scene. Plenty of room should be allowed for characters to walk in front of, behind, and around the manger scene.

*Director's Note: The following scenes can take place with or without breaks. Christmas songs could be sung between the scenes.*

## SCENE 1

*A Christmas carol is played while the stagehand carries out the manger scene and places it on the pedestal. As soon as the stagehand sets the manger scene down, the shepherd speaks the following as a voice-over to the music.*
*Note: The house lights should go out with just a spot on the manger scene during the following monologue only.*

SHEPHERD:    Hey, go easy with the setup, pal. Last year I fell out of this stable, and it was not a pretty sight. *[louder]* Hey, I'm talking to you.

*[Stagehand looks around and isn't quite sure how to respond.]*

All I'm asking is for you to be a little more careful. In case you forgot, we do have a baby in here.

*[Stagehand realizes what might be happening and runs offstage a bit frightened.]*

*[Shepherd directs his voice to the audience as spotlight remains on the manger scene.]*

Look, folks, it wasn't my idea to be here. I was just minding my business, taking care of my uncle's sheep, and now I have to do this manger scene thing every year. *[music underscore begins]* All I am asking for is a few minutes to tell my story, or better yet, this little baby's story. But I can see it is going to be another one of those years. So, welcome to _____ *[name of performance place]* and if you have a few minutes afterward, why not stop by. I would love to chat with you.

*[Music crescendos and lights go off.]*


# SCENE 2

*While a Christmas carol is played on a keyboard or tape, Mr. Director comes from the back of the auditorium and makes his way through the audience, complaining about being late for the performance.*

MR. DIRECTOR:    *[loud and melodramatic]* Oh, I am going to be late for the annual Christmas pageant. What will the church do without me, the director of the Christmas pageant? *[panic-stricken]* And there is still so much to do. I am sure everyone is in a panic. Why, the little lambs and the angels and the shepherds will never make it without me. After all, I am the most important person during this Christmas season.

SHEPHERD:    *[as the director approaches the manger scene on the platform]* Ah, excuse me . . . Hello? . . . Mr. Christmas Pageant Director . . .

MR. DIRECTOR:    *[looking all around for the voice]* Who is saying that?

SHEPHERD:    Hey, I'm down here. . . . Could I have about thirty seconds of your time?

MR. DIRECTOR:    *[still not aware of the source of the voice]* No, I don't have thirty seconds.

SHEPHERD:    Okay, I promise to not take more than twenty seconds.

MR. DIRECTOR:    I don't have two seconds. I have too much to do for Christmas.

[*He hurries offstage, not even noticing the shepherd.*]

SHEPHERD:    [*loudly*] Hey, slow down. . . . [*Mr. Director is gone, speaks to the audience*] See what I mean, folks? Maybe we can try again later.

[*Music picks back up.*]

## SCENE 3

*Mrs. Shopall comes out of the audience with her bags, list, etc. She is also in a frantic hurry trying to get everything done in time for Christmas.*

MRS. SHOPALL:    [*harried and rushed*] Oh, I have so much to do and no time to do it. Now, where was that sale item? [*digging in her purse*] I know I have that five cent coupon. . . . [*worried*] Oh, Mr. Shopall is going to have my head for spending too much money. Now, let's see, last year I spent $7 on Alice, so I better spend $7.25 this year. I just don't know how I am going to do it all. [*stops and faces the audience, near the manger scene, as she holds out her credit cards*] I sure am glad God created credit cards. I'll never leave home without these little wonders.

SHEPHERD:    Excuse me, shopping lady, I have something I would like to share with you. . . . It will only take a minute of your time.

MRS. SHOPALL:    [*looking around*] Who said that? I must be hearing things. I must be going crazy.

SHEPHERD:    I have some really good news for you.

MRS. SHOPALL:    [*cautious*] I don't know who is saying that, but the only good news I could hear is: [*She stands at attention facing the audience, as if to give a speech.*] Attention Shoppers! There is a blue light special in aisle seven by the toy department. [*She hurries offstage.*]

SHEPHERD:    There goes another. By the way, if you folks have any ideas on how I could get someone's attention to hear some good news, I sure would appreciate it.

[*Music plays and lights fade out.*]

## SCENE 4

*As music plays, two teenage girls come walking on stage chatting about everything . . . and nothing.*

TEEN 1:     Did you see that guy parking the Jeep in the lot?

TEEN 2:     You mean the one that looks like he stepped out of Melrose Place?

TEEN 1:     How come we never meet guys that look like that?

TEEN 2:     *[shrugs shoulders and changes the subject]* Hey, what did you get your mom for Christmas?

TEEN 1:     Nothing . . . yet. How about you?

TEEN 2:     Oh, I bought my mom a new blow-dryer.

TEEN 1:     Really? Is that what she wants for Christmas?

TEEN 2:     No, but I need one, so why not . . . share. You know, the Christmas spirit.

SHEPHERD:   *[as the teens near the manger scene]* Hi, ladies, ah, do you have a minute?

TEEN 1:     *[excited]* Did you hear a guy call us?

TEEN 2:     *[equally excited]* Yeah, do you think it's the guy with the Jeep?

TEEN 1:     *[thinking it might be the guy in the Jeep]* Oh, my goodness . . . how do I look? I knew I should have worn my _____ *[name brand]* sweater.

SHEPHERD:   *[as girls walk past the manger scene]* No, it's me, the shepherd from Bethlehem, not Melrose. I'm down here.

*[The girls look at the shepherd and begin to wonder what is going on.]*

I'm sorry, I don't have a Jeep, and I don't care what kind of sweater you are wearing. . . . Really, it doesn't matter.

TEEN 2:     What? It doesn't matter?

TEEN 1:     Of course it matters. *[to Teen 2]* Can you believe that? Let's get out of here.

*[The girls briskly walk offstage believing they are victims of a strange joke.]*

SHEPHERD:   Wow, to think the only good news this year is a four-wheel drive and some crummy sweater.

*[Music plays and lights fade out.]*

## SCENE 5

*Music continues as the businessman makes his way from the audience to the platform, talking on his cell phone. He is upset with the person he is talking to.*

BUSINESSMAN: Look, Bill, can't you get anything right? I told you that the Johnson account is a matter of life and death. We need to close on this before Christmas. That is just four days, Bill! *[louder]* Count them—just four more days. My wife has charged so much money on Christmas gifts that I am going to end up in the poorhouse. I want performance, Bill, and I don't have time to listen to any excuses. I just want to hear some good news!

SHEPHERD: *[excited]* Hey, Mr. Businessman, I have some good news.

*[Businessman spins around looking for the source of the voice.]*

Do you have a minute?

BUSINESSMAN: *[emphatic]* No, I don't have a minute, and what in the world am I listening to? *[looks into manger scene]*

SHEPHERD: Just a simple old shepherd, who spends a lot of time with baby Jesus.

BUSINESSMAN: I can't believe it, a talking manger scene. What will they think of next to get people to buy more Christmas stuff? That is all anyone thinks about, money, money, money. *[hurries offstage]*

SHEPHERD: *[calling after him]* I'm sorry, this really isn't about money. In fact, I don't have any money, just a few sheep and . . . and the Christ of Bethlehem.

*[Lights fade with music softly playing "Silent Night."]*

*Director's Note: It would be nice to move right into the next scene without a break.*

## SCENE 6

*Young Man walks on stage. He does not speak as he walks. He sits dejectedly on the park bench next to the manger scene. Music stops.*

SHEPHERD: Hi, can I talk with you? *[Young Man looks around, saying nothing.]* Down here. I'm the shepherd next to the baby. I'm sorry, I don't have a Jeep or a sweater, but I do have good news for you.

YOUNG MAN: *[looks at the shepherd]* What could possibly be good news today?

SHEPHERD:    Whoa, you've had a bad day, huh?

YOUNG MAN:    *[still addressing the shepherd in the manger scene]* The worst day of my life. *[looks into his cupped hands]*

SHEPHERD:    *[sincere]* Would you care to talk about it? I'm not going anywhere for a while.

YOUNG MAN:    *[holds up a small ring]* Do you see this ring? I had everything riding on this stupid ring. I love her. Maybe you can't understand that, but I love Jenny . . . but I guess she doesn't love me anymore. At least, that's what her note said. You know, she didn't even have the decency to call me on the phone to say we were through. Instead, she sends a card and my—or her—ring back. It really hurts, man, it really hurts.

SHEPHERD:    I'm really sorry about you and Jenny. And, you're right, I can't understand what you are feeling. But, I would sure like to introduce you to someone who does know what you are feeling and really cares. So, if you have a few minutes . . .

YOUNG MAN:    Sure, why not?

*[Music "Silent Night" begins to play and the lights begin to dim.]*

I've got nothing more to lose.

*[Music plays, young man offstage as audience sings "Silent Night."]*

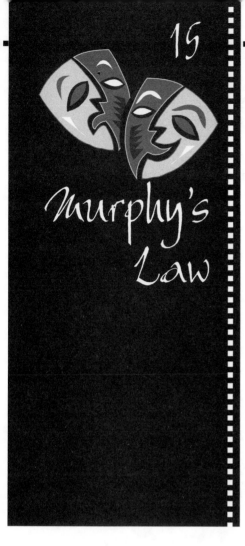

## 15

# Murphy's Law

## THEME

The famous Murphy's Law simply states that if anything can go wrong, it will. That is a truism in life. The problem is not that things go wrong. It is what we do when things go wrong. In this sketch everything goes wrong for Murphy. His response is to deny and then escape from the things that go wrong. He is not willing to admit his problems and deal with them, which is the counsel he receives.

## CHARACTERS

MURPHY: Casually dressed in a very nice sweater as he faces the "day of disaster."

JEFF: Murphy's buddy who tries to encourage his friend to face his problems honestly. He is dressed casually.

MARGO: A doctor and one of Murphy's friends. She tries to encourage her friend to face his problems directly. She is ideally dressed in a doctor's uniform.

VOICE: The voice of a department store intercom.

## SETTING

A department store with a table and sign reading "Clearance Items." A number of items are scattered on the table.

*Music can be playing as Murphy comes on stage and begins to rummage through the clearance items on the display table. Within a few moments, Jeff comes along and bumps into his old buddy, Murphy.*

JEFF: *[cheerful]* Hey, Murphy, how are you doing?

MURPHY: *[rather blah]* Oh, hi Jeff, how are you?

JEFF: *[trying to have fun]* Come on, man, I asked you first.

MURPHY: Ah, fine Jeff . . . just fine.

JEFF: O . . . kay. . . . So, ah, shopping the ol' clearance table, huh?

MURPHY: Yeah, kind of embarrassing. Normally, I wouldn't be caught dead in this section of the store, but, you know . . .

JEFF: So, what has it been . . . about a year since old Goldsmith let you go?

MURPHY: Thirteen months, but who's counting? At least I still have my house.

JEFF: *[painful look he cannot hide]* Yeah . . . right . . . the house. [hand gestures to make* *a roof of a house]* The yellow one on seventh street . . . yours. Nice place, Murphy. *[changes subject]* Hey, Murphy . . . nice sweater you are wearing.

MURPHY: Wait a minute, what was all that about? *[light goes on]* Jeff, you work for the mortgage company that holds the note on my house. You know something I don't know . . . don't you, Jeff?

JEFF: Mr. Richy didn't call you?

MURPHY: The phone never rang. . . .

JEFF: No letter?

MURPHY: The mailbox has been empty. . . .

JEFF: *[bites hand, then speaks very fast]* All right: the bank is foreclosing and you didn't hear it from me.

MURPHY: *[angry]* That two-faced, lying, no good . . . he promised me I had two more months before they would do anything. And I just had a great job interview last week.

JEFF: Sorry, Murphy. . . . *[picks up a vase from the table]* Nice vase, huh?

MURPHY: *[ignoring Jeff]* What could go wrong next?

JEFF: Ah . . . you still have your car. . . .

MURPHY: Yeah, if you want to call it that.

*[Margo enters with a shopping bag.]*

JEFF: *[relieved that the subject and mood can be changed]* Hey, look who's here, Margo Mansfield. How are you, Doc?

MARGO: *[positive]* Jeff . . . Murphy . . . good to see you guys.

JEFF: *[overly friendly]* Great to see you, Margo!

MURPHY: Hi, Margo. *[extends vase]* Need a vase with a chip in it? . . . 50 percent off.

MARGO: Ah, no thanks, Murphy. By the way, how are you feeling?

MURPHY: Fine. . . . *[cautious]* Why? How should I be feeling?

MARGO: Well, I just came from the clinic and saw your chart with the X-rays, and I just thought that . . . you were . . . well, you know. . . . Wait a minute, didn't Doctor Livermore call you?

MURPHY: No call from the Doc, just like *[looks at Jeff]* no call from the bank.

MARGO: Whoa. . . . Well, I'm sorry, Murphy. *[consoling]* I hope they can do something for you.

MURPHY: *[cynical]* Thanks, Margo, you're a real day brightener.

MARGO: *[changes the subject]* Hey, how is . . . what's her name?

MURPHY: Dumped me just after I lost my job. Any other questions before I—die?

MARGO: Not from me. No siree. So, how is the weather for tomorrow's game, guys?

JEFF: *[concerned]* Didn't you hear? El Niño is really kicking up a mess and . . . *[notices Murphy's depression beginning to set in and tries to be cheerful]* . . . and, hey, forget Niño. It should be a great game, right, Murph?

MURPHY: Sure, Jeff . . . sure.

JEFF: *[trying hard to be friendly]* And, remember, you still have your car. A nice red Ford . . . a Galaxy, right? *[aside to Murphy]* By the way, could I have your sweater if you . . . you know, if what the doc says is true. . . .

VOICE: Attention, customers. There is a red Ford Galaxy, license 666DED that has just been hit by a semitrailer in the parking lot. Would the owner of the red Ford Galaxy please come to the service desk?

JEFF: *[notices Murphy's stone look]* Hey, Murphy, no problem, that couldn't be your car . . . not a chance.

MURPHY: *[staring off into space, almost numb]* My car . . . my car.

MARGO: Yeah, Murphy, that could be my car . . . my car is red. It is a Buick, but it's red. You know, it could just be—

MURPHY: Save it, guys . . . just save it. *[stares down at the floor]*

JEFF: Come on, Murphy. You have got to face these things. You know, like coach said in . . . high school . . . pick yourself up and move on. We have a game to win.

MARGO: *[trying to console]* Listen, Murphy, life has bad cards, and you just got a bad hand. And, well, all you need to do is start over. Yeah, that's it, just start over. Something will come together.

*[Murphy begins to walk slowly out of the auditorium, center stage through the audience. Everyone feels his resignation.]*

JEFF:      *[calls to Murphy, loudly]* Hey, Murphy, it could be worse.

MARGO:     *[louder]* Come on, Murphy, bad days come to all of us.

JEFF:      *[even louder]* Murphy, come on back! It's not the end of the world.

MARGO:     Murphy! Life . . . just . . . happens. You know that. . . .

JEFF/MARGO:     Murphy, you can't just run!

*[freeze on stage as Murphy keeps walking; blackout]*

## 16

# Dial-a-God

## THEME

God has written His name on the heart of every person. When special needs arise, we look to God. But many other "gods" get in the way, as we will see in this spoof.

## CHARACTERS

RECEPTIONIST:  A man or woman who is very matter-of-fact about his or her job. She/he is dressed in business attire.

BETHANN:  An adult of any age, dressed up with purse, coat, etc.

BARBARA:  A little older than Bethann, all dressed up and carrying a tire iron.

BILL:  Dressed in a suit or sport coat, tie, briefcase.

BONNIE:  Young and timid, and dressed in casual clothes.

## SETTING

At stage left is a reception desk with a phone and a large notebook. At stage right is a small stand with a phone on it and a sign that reads "Dial-a-God." (Phone dialing sounds and a phone ring would be ideal sound effects for each caller.)

*Receptionist comes out singing "It's a beautiful day in the neighborhood . . ." He/she sits down at desk and begins to read a newspaper with a yawn.*

BETHANN: *[enters stage right, frantically goes to Dial-a-God phone]* Oh, I hope I'm not too late. I just have to get this call in on time. *[scrambling through her purse]* Oh, where is that calling card? I can't believe this AT&TMCISprint to-the-border with thirty-five digits, a wing, and a prayer. *[dials numbers]* This God-thing better work; if I ever needed God, it's now. *[phone on receptionist's desk is ringing and ringing]* I can't believe there is no answer. God must be on vacation.

RECEPTIONIST: *[finally answers, almost annoyed]* Hello, Dial-a-God, state your name, the state you are from, and the kind of god that you need.

BETHANN: Hello, this is Bethann, and I am from Michigan, and I have guests coming over to the house in twenty minutes, and the oven just burned the roast, and my cake went flat, and I need God to help me out.

RECEPTIONIST: *[nonemotional]* How many people do you have coming over for dinner?

BETHANN:        Thirty-five. . . . Just get me in touch with God.

RECEPTIONIST:   Okay, lady, just relax and call 773-2489.

BETHANN:        What?

RECEPTIONIST:   Hey lady, it's the best pizza delivery in town.

[Bethann looks at phone with horror, hangs up, and runs offstage.]

RECEPTIONIST:   Oh, I love my job.

BARBARA:        [enters looking a bit rough and frustrated] A flat tire in the middle of a strange town. Why do these things always happen to me? Life is so unfair, and now I am going to miss my sister's fiftieth wedding anniversary. She is going to kill me. [looks at Dial-a-God sign] Hmmm. Dial-a-God. Now that just might be the answer to my problem. Hey, why not? If God can't fix a flat tire, then who can? [dials number, and it rings]

RECEPTIONIST:   [answers phone] Yeah, Dial-a-God, state your name, city, and request, please.

BARBARA:        Hi, God, this is Barbara from Ohio, and I need you to come out and fix the flat tire on my car, and I would appreciate it if you would hurry. I am going to be late as it is.

RECEPTIONIST:   Whoa, slow down, Barbara from Ohio. This is the answering service, and my job is to simply give you a number to call the god that you need. Now, tell me, where you are stranded?

BARBARA:        [looking around] Ah, by a huge tree with leaves on it, and a white fence, and I think those are cows or maybe horses, and please hurry.

RECEPTIONIST:   Barbara, call Terrific Ted's Tow Truck at 892-4466 and good luck. [hangs up]

BARBARA:        Good luck? A tow truck? What kind of a god? Why, of all the nerve. . . . I can do better myself, thank you very much. [hangs up and stomps offstage]

BILL:           [enters looking a bit haggard and discouraged] After all I did for my company, I can't believe they would let me go. I won more awards in college, I was top salesman of the year for the last two years, and in one foul swoop, fired! [looks at Dial-a-God sign] Huh, now there's a novel idea. God! Hey, what have I got to lose? [dials number and phone rings]

RECEPTIONIST:   [answers phone] Hello, Dial-a-God, name, state, and what do you need?

BILL: I don't know what I need. I just lost my job, and I thought I would give you a call and see if maybe you had some great advice for me.

RECEPTIONIST: *[looking at newspaper]* Have you read your horoscope or Ann Landers today?

BILL: *[a bit surprised]* Well, no, I haven't.

RECEPTIONIST: You ought to. Good stuff today. Anyway, call 451-1122. This guy is a great shrink. You'll like him.

BILL: Hey, wait a minute. I really need to talk to God, not to some $100 an hour psycho-babbler!

RECEPTIONIST: *[defensive]* Hey, pal, nobody talks to God anymore, at least not personally. They call us because they want a quick fix. No one ever calls back disappointed with the advice we give them. They don't need God after we give them the answers they need, so have a good day. Bye.

BILL: Thanks to you, too. *[hangs up phone]* I guess she/he's right. Besides, God's probably too busy to listen to me anyway. *[exits stage]*

BONNIE: *[enters and slowly walks over to the phone, looks at sign, and begins to dial while receptionist speaks]*

RECEPTIONIST: I can't believe how people really think they can get in touch with God when there are so many other great solutions out there. After all, the yellow pages have all the gods they need. *[phone rings, and answers]* Dial-a-God, name, state, and request, please.

BONNIE: *[very timid]* Hi, my name is Bonnie. . . . I don't have to give you my last name, do I?

RECEPTIONIST: Hey, Bonnie, we are on a first name basis around here. Where are you from?

BONNIE: Well, I am from New York, and I'm here visiting my parents. And I have made some terrible choices in my life, and I just feel so . . . guilty and dirty. . . . I was just wondering if you have a god that would be able to forgive me and help me get my life back together?

RECEPTIONIST: *[scrambling through the book]* Forgiveness? *[thinking for a moment]* Have you ever considered prayer?

*[freeze; blackout . . . Music plays them out.]*

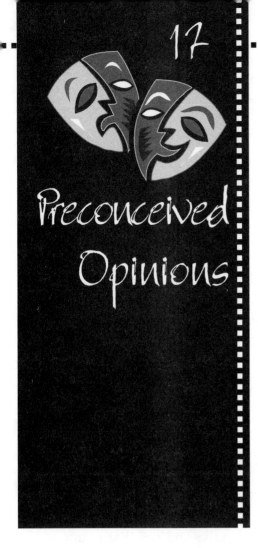

## 17

Preconceived Opinions

## THEME

We are all prejudiced in one way or another. We all have preconceived opinions when we see how people are dressed, or hear their accents, or view the color of their skin. This sketch reveals a subtle prejudice and how it hurts the relationship between two men who attend the same church.

## CHARACTERS

BURT: He has a high opinion of himself and a very judgmental attitude toward others. He is dressed in his Sunday best. Burt cannot tolerate Lloyd.

LLOYD: A reserved, gentle man who does not have a strong view of himself and often feels like the underdog. His less-than-perfect attire (sweater, non-matching slacks, etc.) is far more casual than Burt's. Lloyd really likes and admires Burt.

## SETTING

No stage set is necessary. Both men speak to the audience on opposite ends of the stage. They never interact personally with each other.

*Both men come walking to their positions, prepared to present their case to the audience. Each actor freezes at the end of his line while the other speaks.*

BURT: *[very direct and forceful]* Good evening. My name is Burt Blast, and I am here to set the record straight about Lloyd . . . the loser. So, if you would give me just a moment of your time.

LLOYD: *[rather apologetic, speaks slowly]* Hi, folks. My name is Lloyd, Lloyd Lasiter, but some people call me . . . well, never mind. Anyway, my wife said I need to come here and tell you about my friend, Burt, because she is afraid that you might get the wrong idea.

BURT: The guy is a loser. He can't do anything right. I should have known better when I saw him walk in our church with that ugly _____ *[color Lloyd is wearing on stage]* sweater and slacks from the 1950s. And he has been wearing them every week to church for seventeen years.

LLOYD: *[very kind and sincere]* Burt Blast was the first man I met at church when we came here seven years ago. He was friendly and outgoing. . . . *[smiles]* I really liked that . . . and he made me feel like I was his friend, right from the start.

BURT:    The guy started following me around as if he didn't have a friend in the world.

LLOYD:    At that time I didn't have a friend in the world, and Burt was like a brother I never had.

BURT:    Oh, brother, then the guy shared a testimony in church and told everyone he looked up to me as someone he admires. . . . I could have crawled in a hole.

LLOYD:    I tried to thank Burt publicly one time for the way he made me feel special in church. But, not being good with words and all, I think I said something wrong. He left the church while I was speaking. Actually, he hasn't said a word to me since.

BURT:    And Lloyd drives this dumpy old Chevy with more rust than leaves on a tree, and you can hear that deadbeat's muffler three blocks away. Didn't anyone ever teach the guy the simple basics of auto care?

LLOYD:    I never had anyone to teach me stuff growing up, since it was just my mom, my four sisters, and me. . . . And I thought Burt could be a kind of big brother . . . maybe even a dad . . . to show me how to take care of cars and stuff like that.

BURT:    And did you ever hear the guy speak? [slowly] He talks so slow that you need a calendar to have a conversation with the guy. I have to keep telling him, [loud with exaggeration] "Get to the point, Lloyd. Eternity will come later."

LLOYD:    Burt was a great help to me in my people skills. You see, I was so shy and stuttered real bad when I was growing up. Plus, I couldn't talk to men, having grown up with just women, and that has made my job very difficult, until Burt encouraged me. He would often say, "Get to the point, Lloyd." I really appreciated that . . . and I really learned to talk to my boss. [proudly] In fact, I just got my first raise last week. My boss says I'm showing much more confidence.

BURT:    I am so glad that none of the guys from the club know that I have even talked to the loser. They would revoke my membership. [disgust] I mean the guy lives in one of those subsidized housing units and works for the sanitation department. You know, cleaning up all that . . . stuff.

LLOYD:    [a little excited] Hey, don't say anything, but me and the missus are saving some money to invite Burt and his family over to our apartment for a dinner some time. We are really nervous but kind of excited.

BURT:    The guy was born on the other side of the tracks. I wish he would get a life.

LLOYD:    I know I was born on the wrong side of the tracks. Heard that all my life.

BURT:    *[critical]* Oh, Lloyd is never going to make it.

LLOYD:    *[rejected]* You know, Burt is the first guy that I thought could help me make it.

BURT:    The guy should find another church.

LLOYD:    And you know, I sure love my church.

BURT:    He is never going to fit in around here. He is a source of constant conversation.

LLOYD:    I sure am glad that God brought Burt into my life. He is a source of constant inspiration.

BURT:    By the way, if any of you see the loser, tell him he's at a dead-end.

LLOYD:    By the way, if any of you see Burt, would you tell him I really want to be a good friend?

BURT:    *[beside himself]* How am I going to get rid of this joker?

LLOYD:    *[humble]* How can I ever repay Burt for encouraging me?

BURT/LLOYD:    I guess I'll just have to keep trying.

*[freeze; blackout]*

## 18

## Out Of Focus

## THEME

Sometimes we get off center in our lives and become self-centered. Our sight is drawn to material things and not the things of eternal value and reward. Our two characters have different perspectives. One is focused on godly things, the other on worldly things.

## CHARACTERS

MELISSA: In her twenties, is all caught up in her new fiancé who is Mr. Macho, BMOC (Big Man on Campus). She has totally lost sight of spiritual values. She is dressed casually.

AMY: Also in her twenties, is focused on spiritual things. She tries but fails to help Melissa see what really matters. Dress is casual.

## SETTING

Café table with two chairs.

*Amy is waiting for Melissa, who arrives all excited and full of energy.*

MELISSA: I am so sorry I am late, but *[dramatic]* Amy . . . Amy, Amy, Amy, you will never ever in a million years guess what happened this morning.

AMY: Okay, tell me. What happened?

MELISSA: Well . . . guess!

AMY: But you said I would never be able to guess *[mimicking]* in a million years.

MELISSA: *[playing]* Well, just try. Go ahead, give it your best guess.

AMY: *[playing along]* Okay, *[thinking]* you got a new job.

MELISSA: *[almost out of control]* No, no, no, no, no, no, no. *[giggles]* I told you you couldn't guess. Try again.

AMY: Get control, girl. I am not trying again.

MELISSA: Oh, come on. One more guess and then I promise to tell.

AMY: Just one more?

MELISSA: Give it your best, girlfriend.

AMY: All right, you . . . *[thinking]* got the scholarship you applied for last fall.

MELISSA: I knew you would never get it!

AMY: Tell me what is going on, or I will be charged with homicide in about forty-five seconds!

MELISSA: *[ecstatic]* I'm getting married!

AMY: Say what?

MELISSA: I am getting married!

AMY: Well, it's about time. You and Brad have been dating for three years.

MELISSA: It is not Brad. *[dreamy]* It's Joe Templeton.

AMY: Joe Templeton? *[serious]* Melissa, you better talk to me.

MELISSA: I met Joe six weeks ago at Burger's Galore.

AMY: But you and Brad—

MELISSA: He was there with the entire team after Friday's big game, and he wanted to eat with me.

AMY: But I thought it was forever with Brad—

MELISSA: *[in dreamland]* He will be voted All Conference and will probably be a first round draft pick.

AMY: But you and Brad have dated for three years, and you said—

MELISSA: He is graduating "most likely to succeed."

AMY: *[in her face]* What happened to Brad?

MELISSA: And Joe is so rich. His father is a big-name attorney out east. And why do you keep mentioning Brad? You haven't heard a word I've said.

AMY: No, I guess I haven't. And I am not sure you are hearing a word you have said either.

MELISSA: Just face it, Amy. There was no future with Brad.

AMY: But you guys were perfect together.

MELISSA: If you want to call two school teachers starving in the inner-city perfect . . . or stuck somewhere in the middle of—

AMY: A foreign country? Serving God? That is what you guys had prayed about . . . for . . . for years.

MELISSA: Oh, Amy, we were young and foolish. Now, what kind of life would that be? And how could we raise normal children in the middle of India or Africa?

AMY: But, what about God?

MELISSA: [almost offended] Amy, I still love God and [hesitates] I think Joe will love God someday too. Until then, I am just helping God provide for the future. [dreamy] And what a great future with Joe.

AMY: I can't believe what I am hearing.

MELISSA: Amy, how can you deny good looks, popularity, a guaranteed future, all the money we will ever need? Why, Joe and I can send ten missionaries to Banglemeshiah.

AMY: [disappointed, yet kindly] I just thought you and Brad were so happy, and that God was going to use you to change the lives of others, not just change your own life.

MELISSA: Amy, we need to be practical about these things. God wants us to have the best, you know.

AMY: And Melissa, I thought you had it.

MELISSA: Well, a little extra never hurt anyone, now, did it?

AMY: Maybe not, but I never heard God say that.

MELISSA: Well, I am just being practical.

AMY: Melissa, I think I understand why you don't love Brad anymore. And, I think I understand why you love Joe. But I don't understand your love for God.

[freeze; blackout]

## 19

*Maybe, Just Maybe, He Is Alive*

## THEME

Believers in Christ acknowledge that Jesus rose from the dead. The question remains, "Do I live defeated and discouraged by not appropriating resurrection power?" Or, "Do I live victorious, full of joy, realizing the power of the Resurrection?" This sketch is a first-century scene cast in a modern-day setting.

## CHARACTERS

PHILIP: A downcast disciple of Jesus, casually dressed in twenty-first-century clothes. He is mourning the recent death of Jesus. He is fishing from a bench with his tackle box at his side.

SAMUEL: Philip's friend, also dressed casually. He comes to console his friend Philip.

PETE: One of the twelve disciples, also dressed casually. He is very positive and "up."

## SETTING

A very simple set is in order. A bench/rock creates a fishing spot. This sketch is a story told by eyewitness followers of Jesus, but cast into a modern-day setting. However, first-century clothes and setting could be used.

*Philip enters forlorn and takes a seat stage center and throws out his fishing line. Samuel comes to console.*

SAMUEL: *[to Philip, being rather positive]* Hey, Phil, how's it going?

PHILIP: *[only responds with a nod]*

SAMUEL: *[trying again]* Hey, let me guess. You're fishing.

PHILIP: *[looks and gives a half smile]*

SAMUEL: So, what's with all the chatter? I have never heard you talk so much.

PHILIP: *[ignores Sam and looks in his tackle box]*

SAMUEL: *[sits next to Philip]* Okay, I can be silent. . . . I can just sit here with my friend and watch the world go by. *[pause, looking around]* Nice day for fishing. . . . *[pause]* You know, I could run home and get my pole to join you. *[pause]* If you wanted me to, of course. . . . Yup . . . *[growing agitation]* I could do that . . . yesseree, Phil. *[long pause, slowly looks over to Philip to see if he is responding, finally and directly]* Philip! Would you please tell me what is going on with you?

PHILIP:     *[pause]* I . . . I can't believe He is gone.

SAMUEL:     *[pause]* Look, I miss Him too. But life goes on, and we just have to be tough and move forward.

PHILIP:     Easy for you to say. At least you have a job.

SAMUEL:     *[as if giving a pep talk]* Philip, I think He would want you to be moving upward, forward, always abounding in the—

PHILIP:     Thanks for the speech, coach, but the dreams are gone.

SAMUEL:     Yeah, life could have been pretty exciting. But we can't live in a dream.

PHILIP:     You know, I used to love to fish . . . and now it seems so futile, so empty. It's like nothing matters now. *[leans forward with head in hands]*

SAMUEL:     *[consoling]* Life changes, and life goes on. *[leans forward with head in hands]*

*[Pete enters.]*

PETE:     Hey guys . . . *[sees them both looking miserable]* nice day for fishing. *[no response, tries to be funny]* Let me guess, the sky has fallen, and you guys are carrying the entire world on your shoulders. *[still no response]* Well, you are doing a fine job.

SAMUEL:     What are you so chipper about, Pete? You should feel the same way we do. He . . . He was your friend, too.

PETE:     Oh, . . . now I understand why all the doom and gloom. You guys haven't heard, have you?

SAMUEL:     Heard what?

PETE:     Heard the good news!

PHILIP:     There is no good news today, Peter.

PETE:     *[joyful, with a laugh]* Ha . . . people are already starting to talk. I can't believe you guys haven't heard.

PHILIP:     The only thing that we have heard is that we are finished. Done.

PETE:     Whoa, you haven't heard a thing. *[excited]* Guys, life will never be the same.

SAMUEL:     We already know that.

PETE:     Gentlemen, history is in the making.

PHILIP:      Would you get to the point?

SAMUEL:      Pete, are you on something? Look, don't you have somewhere to go?

PETE:      Sure do, boys. I've got a whole world ahead of me, and it is not on my shoulders . . . *[teasing]* like some people I know.

PHILIP:      Would you tell us what you are so enamored about or . . . or we are going to use you for fish bait.

PETE:      *[Standing over and between them, he speaks very clearly and precisely.]* He . . . is . . . not . . . dead.

SAMUEL:      *[rebuking]* Peter, that is not something to joke about.

PETE:      Guys, He is alive!

PHILIP:      Now you are being disrespectful and . . . and blasphemous. I am not going to stay and listen to this. *[starts to take in his line]*

PETE:      Good. You need to leave and go to the upper room, where we had supper the other night.

PHILIP:      I am not going back there.

PETE:      Fine, suit yourself. But I just saw Him. We ate together. You realize, this changes everything! So, fish if you want, but I am not wasting any more of my time. See ya. . . . *[runs off as he exits]*

*[Philip, without saying a word, begins to pull in his line and makes his way to leave]*

SAMUEL:      Why, the nerve of that loudmouth, arrogant . . . I mean, who does he think we are? I am not stupid. I saw Him die and so did you, Philip. To say that He is alive is . . . preposterous. *[pause]* Hey, where are you going?

PHILIP:      To see the preposterous. If Jesus could raise our friend, Lazarus, then maybe, just maybe, He is alive too. *[hands pole and box to Samuel]* Here, keep this. For some reason I don't think I am going to need it anymore.

*[freeze; blackout]*

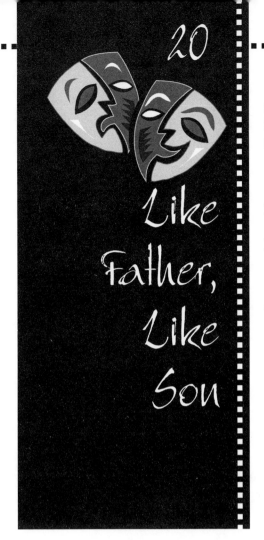

## 20

# Like Father, Like Son

## THEME

Our children mimic us more than we realize. God has called godly fathers to be mentors. A young boy will respond to his father's example, as seen in this sketch.

## CHARACTERS

DON: A laid-back father, dressed very, very casually (sloppy).

DANNY: Don's son, dressed just like his dad.

## SETTING

Two chairs or a couch with junk food and clothes lying all around.

*Don walks out with remote control to watch TV. Danny comes in and stands right in front of Don.*

DANNY: Hey, Dad, can I ask you a question?

DON: *[no eye contact]* Sure, Son, but move over, I can't see the game.

DANNY: Ah, sure Dad, anything you say. *[moves to the side just a little]*

DON: *[into the game]* Look at those _____ *[name of pro sports team]*, boy . . . *[yells]* Go _____ *[last name of a key player on team]*, my man.

DANNY: *[serious]* Ah, Dad? I was talking to my friend Ben, and he said that going to church is a waste of time. And he said our family would be better off just sleeping in on Sunday morning.

DON: *[not hearing a word]* Sure, Son, whatever you say. You can sleep in tomorrow morning; after all, it's Saturday.

DANNY: *[pushing his dad's listening skills]* Dad, Ben says that going to church is for women and sissies.

DON:     Well, I'll tell you _____ [full name of sports hero] isn't a sissy. Look at that instant replay. Boy, you have got to get into this game.

DANNY:   Dad, you haven't heard a word I've said.

DON:     Look, Son, the two-minute warning is coming up . . . five, four, three, two, one. There! We have two minutes to talk. Now, what do you want to talk about? What's bothering you, and make it quick.

DANNY:   Dad, I was asking, why do we go to church?

DON:     Son, I am ashamed that you would even ask.

DANNY:   [saddened] Sorry, Dad, but I really need to know.

DON:     [half serious] Let me give you a little "fatherly" advice, boy. And I am only going to say this once. Your mother would have a fit if we didn't go to church.

DANNY:   That's it? That is the only reason we go to church?

DON:     Well, you know, your grandfather did build the church pulpit, and your grandmother is in the choir every week taking attendance on you and me. So, if we know what is good for us, we will be in church. [tries to be humorous] Get my drift, Son?

DANNY:   Sure, Dad, I think I got your drift.

DON:     Now, Son, you are finally catching on. You are going to make something of yourself sooner or later.

DANNY:   Dad, the pastor said we should have a quiet time. Do you have a quiet time?

DON:     Sure do, Son, every morning when I shave. I hate it when your mother talks to me before I've had my first cup of coffee. Then I can talk.

DANNY:   Dad?

DON:     [showing impatience] Yes, Son. Keep in mind our two minutes is just about up.

DANNY:   Dad, have you ever read through the Bible?

DON:     [scrambling] Ah, now Son, you know some are readers and some are . . . thinkers . . . yeah, thinkers. I think through the Bible.

DANNY:   [doubtful] But how do you think through the Bible when you haven't read it?

DON:      *[scrambling again]* Ah, with prayer and without ceasing. *[pleased with himself]* Yeah, that's it.

DANNY:    *[lightly encouraged]* Ah, so you have a regular prayer time?

DON:      Well, sure I do, and you know I do. Son, we pray before every dinner and then sometimes after, *[jesting]* depending on how good the dessert your mother made was.

DANNY:    Dad?

DON:      Yes, Son, make it quick. The boys are getting back out on the field.

DANNY:    Dad, who do you love more? The _____ *[name of sports team]* or Jesus?

*[Dad looks stunned.]*

*[freeze; blackout]*

# Eternal Choices

## THEME

God's gift of eternal life is just that, a gift. Yet there are many who believe that eternal life is either very costly, or that there is no heaven, hell, or life after death. The views are many. The truth is one.

## CHARACTERS

SAM SLICK: A high-powered salesman who is out to make any deal he can on eternal life. He is dressed in a suit of wild colors.

BILL BUYER: A young, simpleminded person, seeking life in the hereafter. But he has no idea about the truth. He is dressed casually.

## SETTING

Some type of a counter/sales stand from which Sam operates. A large sign reads, "Sale: Eternal Life." He has a notebook and a Bible as props.

*Sam walks out singing, "We're in the money . . ." Bill cautiously approaches the stand, carrying a newspaper ad.*

BILL:    Excuse me . . . ah, I was wondering if you—

SAM:     *[loudly cuts him off]* Wonder no more, my little man. Welcome to our annual sale of eternal life. Shop no more. You have found the fountain of the future, the happy hope, an eternal existence, a guaranteed glory.

BILL:    Well, I was wondering how much this was going to cost?

SAM:     Cost? Why, it all depends on how you want to spend your eternity.

BILL:    You mean I have a choice?

SAM:     Choice is our motto. *[pulls out sign that reads, "Motto: Choice"]* You can choose any eternal plan that you want.

BILL:    I didn't know there was more than one eternal plan.

SAM:     That's the problem with this generation. They don't know all the options. And it is all so simple, my little man.

BILL:    *[eager]* Well then, what are my choices?

SAM:    *[pulls out a notebook to show Bill]* Well, our first one is our most popular option. It is our Reincarnation Reunion.

BILL:    Reincarnation . . . Reunion?

SAM:    That's it, my boy. Just select any one of the people, animals, birds, or insects that you would like to become in your next life, and it will be yours.

BILL:    Well, I don't know how to choose.

SAM:    That is what they all say. But let me make it easy for you.

BILL:    I would appreciate that. This is a big choice.

SAM:    Think no more. What is your favorite food?

BILL:    Steak . . . I love steak!

SAM:    Then you do not want to come back as a Black Angus cow. Now, what was your favorite pet growing up?

BILL:    Ah, Peppy, my goldfish, *[swim action]* really could swim fast.

SAM:    That's it . . . a fish. You will come back as a fish. *[starts to write]*

BILL:    Wait! Could I see the other options before I commit to my next life as a fish?

SAM:    You sure can! Now, let me show you our next popular choice for the next life. We call it the Nirvana Neighborhood.

BILL:    The Nirvana Neighborhood?

SAM:    I hear an echo! Yes siree, kind of a perfect Mr. Rogers world. Everyone is happy, happy, happy, happy . . . and connected to whatever they believe is spiritual. This is our spiritual buffet special, where you can create your own life hereafter. You can have it your way.

BILL:    Wow . . . I bet it is rather expensive.

SAM:    You don't get a perfect life for nothing, my friend. So, if you would like to sign your life away right here, *[coughs]* I mean, sign on the dotted line, we will bill you later.

BILL:    Well, I don't know. What are the guarantees?

SAM: Guarantees on eternal life? Think about it, Son. There are no guarantees at the hospital, or at your job, or even in your relationships. *[pushing to close the deal]* Now, just sign here.

BILL: You said there were several options. Are there any more?

SAM: Well, I don't think you would be interested in the other two we have on sale.

BILL: Well, try me. I'm not convinced of the others.

SAM: Can you spell nihilism? You know, the doom and gloom story, big-time judgment, fatalism, condemnation, end of the story, end of the line—not a fun picture, take my word for it. Not a popular way to go from this life, if you know what I mean.

BILL: Whoa . . . but you mentioned you had two more. What's the other option?

SAM: Well, let's call it our least popular option. Not too many people go for this one.

BILL: Actually, I want to hear about it.

SAM: Of course you would. It is called Heaven or Hell. It is an ancient belief, and it is all found in this book. *[holds up a Bible]*

BILL: So, how does it work?

SAM: Well, I am told you read this book, believe what it says, and then hope.

BILL: Hope?

SAM: Yes, hope! Say, why don't you just admit with me that this life is it, that there is no hereafter, and I will give you a great deal on a vacation package in Florida.

BILL: *[picks up the Bible and wants more answers]* You said, "Hope." Hope for what?

SAM: Hope that what is said in this book is true. Like I said, not popular.

BILL: *[holding the Bible]* So, who wrote this book?

SAM: God did. At least, that is what everyone says.

BILL: Great. I'll take it!

SAM: Are you sure?

BILL:    No, I'm not sure. But I am sure that God knows, and I think He is more reliable than the rest of these.

SAM:    *[exasperated]* One in every crowd.

*[freeze; blackout]*